SMITTEN
This Is What Love Looks Like

Poetry by Women for Women
An Anthology

Indie Blu(e) Publishing
Havertown, Pennsylvania

SMITTEN This Is What Love Looks Like

For information, address
Indie Blu(e) Publishing
indiebluecollective@gmail.com

ISBN: 978-1-951724-00-9
Library of Congress Control Number: 2019916930

Editors:
Candice L. Daquin
Hallelujah R. Huston

Cover Design:
Mitch Green

Dedication

To the generations of women before us, who suffered for their love without recourse.
We who exist today inherit the voices of all women who have loved women.
Never silence your heart.

Praise for SMITTEN

"This is poetry that penetrates into the heart of not only the experience of lesbian love, but into what love means to the human psyche. These are emotions that live in each of us; that they are expressed here with a uniquely feminine interpretation truly enriches the palette of lesbian literature.

Women poets have here found a stage upon which they can present their passions and intimate feelings openly and in unison. *SMITTEN* brings the beauty and intricacies of women's love for each other into a unique and captivating presentation. With the publication of this volume, Indie Blu(e) remains at the forefront of giving lesbian literature a new and important direction.

Lesbian writers have long suffered the neglect of history and the close-mindedness of the world of literature and have yet somehow managed to rise above the indifference and the prejudice to express their distinctive creativity. The women represented in *SMITTEN* are strong voices confidently expressing their individuality. Perhaps Sappho verbalized it best when over two thousand years ago she wrote:

"*May I write words more naked than flesh, stronger than bone, more resilient than sinew, sensitive than nerve.*"

Yes, that is the kind of poetry to be found within the pages of *SMITTEN*."

-Erik Klingenberg

"Candice Daquin and the editors at Indie Blu(e) Publishing have worked their magic once more in raising a powerful chorus of voices. . . even though *SMITTEN* is not exclusive, it must be recognised as an anthology paving a new way for literature. All of the writers are female and all of the subject matter is female, lesbian, bisexual and more. Pieces such as 'Lesbian' by Avital Abraham and 'Pulse' by

Melissa Fadul drive home why Daquin's decision to create a collection like this is needed and welcomed.

It is possible people will read the sub-heading of *SMITTEN* and assume this is an exclusive collection; only accessible if you are woman who loves or has loved a woman. But, what is truly wonderful is this isn't true at all. Instead, *SMITTEN* holds and nurtures love poems to be read and enjoyed by anyone. After all, for centuries, we have consumed and enjoyed love poems written about women, by men. Why should the fact that the poet is a woman cause the response to be any different?

Too often we sideline LGBTQ+ work as a genre of its own, when it should be mainstream; literary works which are written by people to be enjoyed by people, no matter what their race, sexuality, gender and/or religion.

Yet, until this happens, I applaud Daquin and Indie Blu(e) Publishing for brazenly making a stand. Until labels are but words and not identifiers, it is important that writers like those in this collection share their voices and stories, ever-lasting love and heartbreak, and their hopes and fears, to remind the literary world they *will* be heard, no matter what the response may be."

-Kristiana Reed, *Between the Trees*

"Here are 263 facets of the jewel called love (I counted). No, this is not a collection only for women. This is rich poetic food for humans who love, who have loved, and who hope to love."

-Robert Wertzler

"Although this is subtitled "Poetry by Women for Women", to assume that this is only relevant to women who love women (or even only to women at all, leaving out male readers) and to pass it by because of that would be a terrible mistake. At its center, it is simply about love, experienced and expressed by an eloquent and diverse collection of writers, of all ages, from all backgrounds, viewpoints and walks of life.

That it focuses on women loving women is important to address because of the stereotypes, bigotry and discrimination that exists in our society. The battle to love whom we choose is one that shouldn't even have to be fought in 2019, but unfortunately still is. The writings within Smitten elicited from this made me want to weep. It makes me sad that such a heartfelt plea as “Love Not Hate”, for example, imploring society to accept people as they are even needs to be said today.

But the underlying emotions are relatable to anyone who has ever fallen in or out of love. The joy of finding that person who completes you, the feeling of instant connection, the passion, as well as the searing grief when a relationship ends are shared experiences for most everyone, and that is what this book is all about. The variety of work within Smitten is wide, and runs the gamut of feelings from the lowest point of loss and rejection to the ecstatic highs of those moments in life of pure happiness, and it showcases some truly exquisite writing. It is obvious that these come from the heart, from lives lived – the voices are real and must be heard.”

-Karen Herman

“As I formed my thoughts, I realized that I was (and am) extremely nervous about how to respond to these poems from my own heterosexual, cis-woman lens. I felt this because I am a woman of color, one who feels the simmering heat of frustration when those who cannot ever know my experience want to take a stab at relating to it. And as I read and re-read, I felt and understood that what I can say is the following: While Smitten is a book about women who love women (from every-which perspective), of course, it is about *love.* And I can relate to love. I can understand first love, last love, forbidden love, unrequited love, the love of someone lost, the love of someone found. The love of someone who saves.

But in truth, even as a woman of color married to a white man, I have not experienced love that is criticized or fetishized by outsiders, that is closeted by well (and not-so-well) meaning family. I will never feel the excruciating pain of those who are beat down because of whom or how they love. So, as I opened up my advance copy of Smitten, it was with delicate hands, an open and reverent heart—because that is how I wish my own poetry to be read.

Over a hundred poems about women, by women. Can I say how exhilarating it is to have read so many at one go? I happily recognized quite a few of the poets—hailing from an independent poetry network often curated by Indie Blu(e) Publishing. . . there was (also) a mélange of poets new to me, whose unique voices were employed in a variety of styles from musical to prose to concrete poetry.

Would that I could list every single poem (my list is long), as they touched my sensibilities in different ways. Some entreat us to dance to an inaudible tune; others confide to us the secrets of nerve-wracked first kisses; they relate the early-in-the-morning and late-at-night mundanities of love. But we are also invited to the troubled history of these loves in poems such as "Love is Our Theory" (Sean Heather K. McGraw), "Letter from Lock Up to the NYPD, June 1969, Christopher Street" (Melissa Fadul) and "You Don't Deserve to Read About My Life" (Georgia Park). These such poems are the ones that will be hardest to bear, but among the most important to read.

This is a book that should be gifted. In spite of its implied audience, *Smitten* is not just for women who adore women. It is for those whose hearts twist and skin prickles at romance, who know the flight of butterflies in their stomachs, who long for the feeling of home in another's heart."

-Mariah Voutilainen

“Love doesn’t have just one “look” to it and I thank SMITTEN for reminding readers of that.

Love transcends race and gender.”

- Christy Birmingham, *Versions of the Self*

Preface

You hold in your hands a collection of deeply felt words by women who have unapologetically loved another woman, and *this matters*. A woman loving another woman romantically and passionately is a revolutionary act; it is even more so when such a woman commits those feelings to paper, exposing themselves in a way most lesbian and bisexual women cannot imagine doing in real life. How thrilling, and how terrifying it would be to open a window, and scream the title of Carolyn Martin's superb poem, "I Love You More than Mariska Hargitay". Or to walk the halls of a typical American high school whispering teenage phenom Clementine's sweet, earnest plea "Please Like Girls".

At its heart, this collection of writing is all about love, which we believe all readers can relate to and appreciate. Who among us has not fallen in or out of love, or longed for an unrequited love? Our advanced readers, male and female; lesbian; bisexual; gay; and straight confirmed our hypothesis. All of them expressed the sentiment that love is love and that it transcends categories, labels and clichés. Anyone who is open to appreciating love and poetry can gain as much from this collection of poems as a lesbian can.

We believe that these lesbian and bisexual voices are necessary in this predominantly heterosexual world, where most publishing is still male-orientated, and our ideas of relationships are dominated by the male lens.

Before the internet, lesbians had to find inventive ways to meet one another. In the 1950's, women talked about furtive meetings in shady back street bars that used special code words because the fear of police raids was ever looming. While lesbians and women who love women have come a long way since those days, in part thanks to the World Wide Web and the opening up of what was once secret, there still remains a neglected history of what love between women really feels like.

Very few of the contributors to this volume had literary role models to draw on as they grew into their sexual identity. Today, a significant amount of lesbian and bisexual literature is either erotic or found in the Mystery/Detective genre. Traditionally, passionate relationships between women have been invisible, misunderstood, or minimized. When acknowledged, these relationships have often been fetishized for the straight male gaze, or ended tragically in a cautionary tale for any young woman who suspected her own romantic attraction to other women.

We have longed to read authentic expressions of love and emotion between women but such a volume did not seem to exist. We knew that these voices existed in the writing community, and the tireless Candice L. Daquin dedicated herself to finding them. At first, submissions came in as a trickle. Then gradually, word spread about the project. We had absolutely no idea when we began that we would receive so many submissions and would end up with this magnificent, 120+ contributor book.

If we allowed ourselves, could we locate our own lives in A. Lawler's "You, Vodka" or Paula Jellis' "I Want a Woman with a Big Bouffant"? Would we be willing to feel as deeply as Crystal Kinistino must have when she wrote "The Burned Out House We Inhabit"? As women in a modern, over-stimulated world, we believe many of us shy away from feeling too much, too deeply, too often. Poetry defies this retraction, and as women-loving-women poets we delve into dark, delicious and dangerous places.

SMITTEN is a book so many of the contributors would have been happy to find on the shelves when we were coming out and we hope everyone who reads it walks away moved by the nuance and shading the contributors have painted the many facets of love in.

Let us then celebrate these women who felt, who wrote, who submitted, and willingly exposed themselves as openly loving women. It is not easy. Loving honestly and authentically is a revolutionary way of being, and committing it to the page may well outlive ourselves. We salute first-time published poets, such as Dr.

Snehn Rooh and Olivia Chahinsky, as well as the veterans, including Jessica Jacobs and Sarah Bingham, who come out (again) in defiance of a world which often does not want to feel or hear or know of women loving women.

Lastly, we are be mindful of how many countries still exist where homosexuality is illegal or socially unacceptable. Let's consider for a moment all the women and men who remain silently suffering, their true natures hidden, because they have no protection or safe place to go. Projects like this give a voice where a voice is able to be given and every voice helps break down the walls of bigotry, hate and intolerance and assists future generations from having to endure those prejudices.

Candice Louisa Daquin
Hallelujah R. Huston
Kindra M. Austin
Christine E. Ray

Acknowledgements

Many thanks to Kristi McKenzie, Mariah Voutilainen, Alicia Sophia and Jill Blake for your invaluable input and help.

All the wonderful SMITTEN reviewers who were kind enough to read advance copies.

Special thanks to Christine E. Ray and Kindra M. Austin of Indie Blu(e) for supporting the idea and realization of SMITTEN. Without publishers like you, the world would be monochrome.

Contents

Lesbian
Avital Abraham

There are many dirty words in this world,
but the one that I have come to hate most of all
is lesbian.
Because lesbian feels like my mother
telling me I don't need labels yet,
because I'm still young,
and there's still time;
I could still end up with a man.
Lesbian sounds like her dry, uncomfortable laugh,
choking on the graves of grand babies
that will never find a home in my womb;
I'm sorry mama.
Lesbian feels like the elephant in the room,
the lump in my throat,
like we know you're gay,
but do you have to be ... gay?
Like not so casually, casually dropping into conversation,
"Yeah, my ex-girlfriend...",
like glancing at faces with scripted smiles,
"Oh, well you know I totally support you,
I went to pride march in New York last spring
so I completely get your
lifestyle."
Lesbian is loneliness,
piling on the couch
sleeping bags pulled up to our chins, Nicholas Sparks and Cinderella
dancing across the screen.
The guy gets the girl;
the girl gets the guy and they all live
happily
ever
after.
Lesbian is not on the screen,
and lesbian will never have

happily
ever
after.
We will only have a fear of holding hands and safe distance,
drenched in the knowledge that
this kind of love is not the right kind of love.
Lesbian tastes like shame,
and copper
and coming out again and again,
and hoping,
and praying
that those words will not be my last words.
Lesbian tastes predatory,
like a lion stalking its prey,
hiding in the grasses,
hiding in casual conversations with friends,
hiding in browser histories.
Lesbian is a monster.
Am I the monster?
Because oh,
oh god,
do I want that word to feel delicious.
I crave its comfort,
dream about snuggling into the word lesbian,
like lesbian I'm coming home,
and lesbian warm smiles,
lesbian lazy mornings and,
lesbian a fluffy duvet,
lesbian half coffee, half cream, two sugars.
Lesbian, lesbian, lesbian,
and it still feels dirty in my throat but -
lesbian -
I will keep saying this word until - lesbian -
it burrows its way into my brain and
lesbian makes a home on my tongue.
I will not let this word be dirty

Testimony
Carolyn Martin

When she argues in absolutes,
there's no defense.
You never ... I always ...
(she declaims in perfect pitch)
... vacuum rugs upstairs.
        ... lock the sliding door.
                ... sing a song on key.

I confess I'm tonally inept
and prone to chronic laziness.
I'd rather watch the sun unfurl
behind our evergreens

than lug the Kirby up the stairs,
unwind its twisted chord, and miss
the smatterings of crumbs and lint
she always finds.

As for the sliding door,
chalk it up to trust in Providence
and patio debris I've scattered
as a trap. Any thief who'd plow
through rakes, hoes and piles
of leaves deserves a chance.

Since there's no gain in wasting breath
nor expiration date on being wrong,
I've mastered shutting up and dreaming
of the rainy night she cannot find her
keys and kettledrums each bolted door,
while high above the vacuum's hum,
I'm belting out her favorite songs
from the second floor.

(Previously published in *Persimmon Tree*)

Letter from Lock Up to the NYPD, June 1969, Christopher Street

Melissa Fadul

I was the first woman who threw a stone at your head before you shackled me. Do you remember me pleading, *can you please loosen the cuffs—they're cutting into my wrists*. You spotted blood on your hands, cracked me over the skull with your baton in one swift blow and yelled, *stop bitchin.*' I looked up at our stars that seemed to be weeping light. Red stripes painted your forehead. You shoved me in to the back of the patrol wagon, and wiped your face on your uniform sleeve near your upside-down badge.

A brook of blood dropped, mixed and gelled with mine when it hit the floor after you slammed the door and turned me into a witness.

I bowed my head, unable to watch one more cop throw another lesbian face first against the car. One more body thumped like thunder against the steel and my head couldn't help but throw itself up and peek through the window—There were these eyes—ones that met mine— I couldn't distinguish sweat from her tears—even water wasn't free. Hydrogen and oxygen couldn't escape labels. She stared at me so long and hard, her irises morphed to swords, ready to cut a portal in me—a time machine to the future.

I kicked in the door with my heels to divert attention from her—the cop continued his frisk. She wailed over and over, *that is me! That is me*!—even after he spit on her chest while screaming, *then why is there a man in the picture? Why the fuck are you wearing a dress?* The ID fell—she bounced against the paddy wagon once more. With her cheek and ear flushed against the window, he threw her arms and hands to the glass and spread her legs. I whispered, *mercy* and imagined my hand free to press against hers.

I Want a Woman with a Big Bouffant

Paula Jellis

I want a woman
with a big bouffant
cat eye glasses
and a sassy walk
hot pink hot pants
and a leopard print top
a skin tight dress
showing all her curves
who loves to dance
and loves big words
I'd love to give her all
she deserves
like respect.
Warm hands
strong fingers
soft lips
that know...how to linger
when we go for a ride
to Venus or to Mars
in the countryside
with fireflies and stars
a woman who likes to tango
polka...mambo...and cha-cha-cha
ooooo la la!

I want a woman
who wants a woman
like me
in a flannel shirt
or bvd's
or big ol' boots
or a three-piece suit
Listening to jazz
staying up 'til 2

laughing and loving
the whole night through
If you want a woman like me,
I want a woman like you

Reclamation

Crystal Kinistino

You with your moonstone mood,
your chameleon heart,
a worn keepsake
from a time when love unlocked the door,
as I have locked you out--yet still
continue to keep you w/in a finger's reach

You, at the crux of lower medulla,
your kick of solar plexus
a melancholia of sexual appetite,
that oxycotin/oxytocin capsule of my need,
with her moon in Aquarius,
and her Scorpio rising

You, who remind me of a walk on the beach,
your hand outreached
with sun-bleached capillaries
that burn me in their venous return

You, who remind me of those we crawl into,
through the loneliness of abalone shells
with their pearl-essence of
punctured palms, torn alabaster

You, the earth bastard with your home-sick ache
traveling through circular nerves,
the cobalt snake of my rami-communicans,
your splanchnic & adrenal pathways
sinking back into the red cerebral sea of me

This is how you occupy me;
at the abandoned
alter of my sacrificial childhood,
a home not meant to be inhabited,

an unmarked grave of forced embraces,
with the thrill of hand on thigh,
swallowing me alive
at the cyclone of the mother eye--
where entering you I reclaim myself.

Please like girls
Clementine

First off
I really hope that you like girls
But then again you seem to be into musicals and stuff
And theatre tends to attract the gays

I really hope that I'm your type
Cause I've never before met someone whose mine
Every time you glance at me (which is a lot)
I kinda feel like I'm 'bouta die

Honey o, honey o, please please
Please just like me
Even if it's unlikely
I'll give myself hope
I'll be prayin askin hopin you like girls
Girls like me
Just say to me
"I like girls"

The way you do your makeup
Gets me smilin away
It's a style only you could pull off
You finished my stupid reference
When no one cared
To be honest, it made my heart stop

And everything seems more intense than
When it really happened
When I dwell on the events of the day
You're the rain to my thunder
You're the cookies to my milk
I just hope that you're bi or gay...

I mean we've shared a couple words

This Is What Loves Looks Like

You seem pretty cool
You make the workload hurt a bit less
Your face makes my feelings a whirlpool

I see the way you glance at me
A lot more than people do normally
There's no hate or grimace in those stares
Dear my girl
Do you really care?

I'll try to be a bit less anxious
Maybe talk to you a bit more
This is a stupid, dumb love song
But it's cause you warm me to the core

Cause
Honey o, honey o please please
Please just like me
Even if it's unlikely
I'll give myself hope
I'll be prayin askin hopin you like girls
Girls like me
Just say to me
"I like girls"

Oh seriously this isn't funny anymore
My heart and mind are getting real sore
I really don't wanna be such a bore
But mi amor
Please like girls

In the Grove of Self-Charging Trees
Jessica Jacobs

"Darling do you remember
the [one] you married? Touch me,
remind me who I am."
—Stanley Kunitz

It is early enough that fog still skeins
the highest branches.
And twining each tree: a cable
rough-creped as wild grape vine,
with both ends socketed
into the trunk. Murmur and fizz
of power pulled from the sky,
from the earth—power recirculated
by the cables, nothing wasted.

In a clearing
no bigger than our cabin's double bed, you spread
a blue blanket. We make a picnic
of a peach and a plum. Then, with no top sheet, no
clothes, not even a bracelet—How long has it been,
love, since we touched? Even
our kisses are given
on the way to something else.

Yet here, our bodies
do not just tighten but seal
fast around the other and we
kiss the kind of kiss that's like entering
a glass cathedral, a structure that exists
to emphasize the space it contains
while leaving visible all it does not.
We move
into that kiss as we move

into each other—with gentle
force, a matched insistence—
and all the trees begin to hum. Self-charging circuits,
all of us, drawing from the world
a stream of heat and light, which we pass between us
like a fire that burns but does not consume.

I wake to your back; your body
an early-morning house in which all the inhabitants are still
asleep, the lights extinguished, the doors locked and bolted. Yet
beside our bed, the marigolds you brought me
burn like paper caught in the act of ignition, orange and red
petals of flame. And on each of our ring-fingers, the same
silver band: my promise to you,
my charge, that through the forest and fog, through
the busy thicket, I will
never stop finding my way
to your door. All I need from you
is to answer;
all you have to do is let me in.

You/Vodka

A. Lawler

I’m not sure who I love more
You or vodka.
And here we are, the three of us tonight.
You undo your hair and let it drape down your shoulders.
I could tell you all night how gorgeous you are. But then again, I’m a few drinks past sober.
I’ll tell you everything and more.
I swore I wouldn’t.
But I knew I couldn’t keep my word.
I’ll pray in the morning that you still love me the way you seem to now.
I’m buzzed, and vodka makes me happy, so over 12 dollar drinks I might be talking a little too
loud.
I’ve explained in loose details
Who I am and how I love.
It’s tough to say the words, but I’m nothing if not a confident drunk.
I know I won’t take you home tonight. I’m okay with that. You hand over your lip-gloss and tell
me to try it and I do.
It’s not like me. I’m neurotic and self-conscious and generally a buzzkill. But I’m not me when
I’m with you.
I’ve decided that I don’t need to see the wonders of the world. I just need to memorize your
tattoos.

Shifting Sand

Tia M. Hudson

Drive on the sand,
It will be OK.
I told you about times
I drove forward with care.
You felt it shift beneath us;
you wanted to stop
No, I said. Just keep going;
it will be fun.
Here and now we sink
with a beautiful view
that we cannot move toward.
I kneel by the car, digging.
You let the dogs out
for a quick run down the beach
I call the tow truck
as the tide comes in.

Walking by Hot Topic while announcing Queerness, or so I hoped

Kelsey Hontz

The mall—
Adolescent playground,
Soaked in sugar body spray because
Only younglings want their skin to smell like a cupcake,
Delectable, better to look at than to touch.
Us stepping out in our character shoes,
The theater kids thrust upon the real world on the rare Saturday
When there was no rehearsal.
She was the odd one out,
The teen with no awkward phase,
The one who did not have to wear braces like medieval armor,
Acne like her very own name,
Stretchmarks and uneven breasts like a costume that would hang
Incorrectly for the next six years—
She was perfect.
(And not just through my ill-corrected glassy eyes but
to anyone who looked upon her)
A Snow White come to technicolor life, curtains of dark hair
Framing alabaster skin that nonetheless stretched into a smile
When she looked at me. (Me!)
She said to me,
"Let's hold hands and walk around the stores!"
And so we did, her cool hand in mine,
Which I'm sure was so slippery with sweat
If it were salmon a bear would catch it and immediately throw it back,
Because something was wrong with it. Too nervous.
And she said,
"Look at the way they're looking at us.
They hate to see two girls holding hands."
I felt defiant and strong and brave as she
Turned up her nose at

The older women walking into Torrid to buy themselves stretch pants and
We felt invincible.
My eyes have worsened through the passing of the years, but looking back is clear.
To me, that was formative—
How it was to be seen with another woman in public
To her, it was
Per formative—
Another show to put on when the playhouse was closed
I had won the best role yet,
And she
Could do better.

Aubade under an Overpass or Stumbling into the only Gas Station

Piper Michelle

After several deer
contemplate the prospect of suicide
by means of my Scion;
the mirrors behind their eyes glinting
follow-me tails turned up
I start to forget what your hand feels like in mine.
*
A cotton market bag
passed between us
like an infant in flood waters,
we crumpled ourselves
over the logs
the ocean churned out.
Unfolded our limbs
like the undulations
of an anemone.
The weight of our bodies
pressed salt-water out of the sediment
put silt on my spine;
we unmade our bed on that beach.
Under the covers of your button-down
buttoned-down,
missing the button between your breasts.
My mouth yearned for your nipple.
I made a nest for you in my body.
In the Sand-Dune Bar all plaid
baseball-capped
work-booted women,
asked what dildo we use
where to get laid
if we knew Prince came here 3 times a year.
Pierced right-ears
shaved heads and cleavage

baroque lace and sweat,
our people
said fuck you to the bathroom signs
and fucked in the bathrooms.
We siphoned oxygen through the hourglass
unbalanced between our chests
it filled as it emptied
the juice in the punch-bowl under my tongue
spilled over your teeth
grew lichen on our gums.
We passed towns with names that must have begun as a joke
until someone made a sign
and another one after the first was stolen—
3 towns
10 gas stations
all closed.
The edge of Portland echoed
in my ears
6 dollars on pump 2
a man predicted my death
finger pointed at my forehead
called me faggot.
*
I will not cease and desist my identity
manacle my mouth
turn my queer cheek.
Your disappointment aches in the fingers that loosen around my hand.
How the rosemary bushes in your front yard
quiver their goodbye.

You Don't Deserve to Read About My Life

Georgia Park

Mother, if you are reading this
wondering why you are excommunicated
let me remind you
of where the trouble started, at least
I was either twelve or thirteen
suffering from depression
and you refused to believe my diagnosis
or honor my prescription
and then I finally made a friend
which you were fine with
until you heard we were running around
holding hands
you picked me up from the mall that weekend
with a suitcase packed in the backseat
and said my father would take care of me
that you couldn't do it
you said it's not enough that I cut my classes
but now I have to be a lesbian on top of it
it's not like I was a good kid to begin with
and that you couldn't deal with this
shortly after, I think
I cut my wrists and shaved my head
at my new school in the hillbilly region
they called me some names
I can't bring myself to mention
tried to force me to kiss a girl
at the dance
and when I hit them
they hit back
so I stopped going
my father would drop me off at the office
and I would wander into the woods after second period
so my father gave me up to live with my then girlfriend
because he also couldn't handle this

…I still can't talk about
what happened next
but I have no interest in ever
repairing our relationship
So mother, if you are reading this
stop it.

I will not be another flower

Erin Van Vuren

I will not be
another flower,
picked for my
beauty and left
to die. I will
be wild, difficult
to find, and
impossible to
forget.

- Erin
Van Vuren

The Queen of Spain

Hallelujah R. Huston

That cashmere
dress I bought you
which you never wore
price tag molten now
the ink of its exorbitant cost
smudged off

Did you think yourself
too femme in it
too glamorous
too small?

The rape left you
exposed
too much being female
to want touch
even from another
woman

I saw you healed
and restored
not as a hole
filled by hatred

The caress of its
delicate electric
purple fibers draped
regal upon
your shoulders,
the black crown of
your Catalan hair
worn high
No man's greed could
ever spoil you,

mi amor
no horrific afternoon
trapped in an attic
in Madrid could
ever lessen your grace,
mi reina.

Her Voice
Marie Prichard

A woman, once invisible Standing right here, at this point in time Slightly altered— yet still the same, Heard her voice say, "I see you."

A woman's experiences entwined into the core of her being Whispering secrets about life's exquisite moments, Heard her voice say, "I hear you."

A woman awakened, moved beyond complacency Eyes no longer closed, no longer sleepwalking Moving through time and space, Heard her voice say, "I recognize you."

A woman, evolving A butterfly poised to emerge, to take wing Not finished— not even close, Heard her voice say, "I believe in you."

A woman, an effigy of a female, a sculpture, a carving A mold created and meant to be adored Finally able to be loved completely; cherished irrevocably, Heard her voice say, "I want you."

A woman touched, a brief caress across her cheek The waxing and waning moon forever pulling and releasing the tides, Heard her voice call her name.

An Exchange Quick and Quiet

Christine E. Ray

you held me
in tender embrace
in your deepest heart
we lived together
laughed together
dreamed together
breathed together
unfathomable
that anyone
could take my place
it was an exchange
quick and quiet
waking up alone
stripped of you
of our imagined future
a featherless
newborn bird
raw, pink
awkward
unsteady
heads turn
away from me
ugly in my grief
unsightly in my pain
I am no martyr
but the loss of us
steals my breath
drags me underwater
seeks to drown me
threatens disintegration
no room yet
for shiny toothbrushes
on the bathroom sink
unfamiliar tee shirt

hanging behind the bedroom door
or poetry written to new eyes

I'll Be Seeing You

after Billie Holiday

Maria Gray

Knees red and dry with Martian dust, you
stretch your silver arm out towards the sun.
Whatever you are looking for, I hope you find
it, cradled by the crater, untouchable and new. You
build yourself a house atop the moon
and never leave your window during the night.

This chokehold swath of dark is long, the night
endless and insufferable. Through my binoculars, you
prepare breakfast, prove your bread that swells like moons
and eat it alone with nobody to take care of the leftovers. No son,
no daughter. You are old and alone and all too new,
sweet Opportunity, engineered to find

light on the dark side of a planet strange and lifeless, find
sweet, strange fruit mummified in rocky soil. This night
is long and lonely. This I know. I want to wake up new
as much as you. I want to talk to you,
honey. We have so much in common, orbiting the same sun
like it's nothing. I mean nothing to the moon

and she is all I see. The sweet, indifferent moon
means everything to me. Nowadays, I find
myself wondering how you do it, biting the sun
that feeds you, befriending the unholy night,
making peace with your holey robot heart. You
are born again each morning, thin-skinned and new.

I leave my bed, reluctant, heart beating pink and new
and furious, half-dark and impartial like the moon.
You are a warrior. Never forget. I salute you
and your boundless courage and loneliness. I find
they often occupy the same coin. At night,

the sky is open-stomached, white and burning as the sun,

unconscious and close-eyed on a hospital table. The sun
does nothing but what she has grown to know. Today is new
and we have finally reached it. This purple, bruised night
will only pass once, swollen as the moon,
equally devoid of answers. In the book of hymns, we find

a mournful Billie song and bid goodnight to you:

I'll find you in the morning sun,
and when the night is new,
I'll be looking at the moon but I'll be seeing
you.

Muse
Wandeka Gayle

If I could capture this peace
spread it out with the base of a spoon

warm and pliable like stewed June plums,
I would, dear heart.

I would scoop it up with both hands
or let our fingers slide into the wet,

together feeling every residue of the fruit

If I could preserve this glimpse of happiness,
make it linger, I would, love.

I would extend this making, examine every morsel
before I bring it to my lips.

Carol
Susie Fought

I am sitting on the floor of your room drinking peppermint tea. You are sitting on your bed sorting through a stack of records. Leonard Cohen is singing Suzanne takes you down to the place by the river. I look at the album cover. Dark bushy hair. Black turtleneck. He looks like you. Your room is tiny. When you cross to the record player I can feel your breath. Your voice makes me dizzy. You teach English grammar to the boys at the priory where you live. You drink Benedictine and smoke cigars with the monks. I am jealous. I don't want you to enjoy anyone but me. Your closest friend is my lover. You have a boyfriend named Trevor and you talk about him as if you hate him. I sit there on your floor, leaning against your bed, waiting for you to kiss me. You bring me another cup of tea, step over my legs, and sit down on the bed inches from my shoulder. I can smell your new Levis, the damp wool of your turtleneck, your Benedictine breath. Your black hair is curly and cut like a boy's. You have Portuguese grandparents. You wear brown loafers with pennies in the cuffs. You talk endlessly about Trevor. I watch your mouth move. I try not to imagine you in bed with him. My stomach aches. Leonard Cohen sings about loss and loneliness. My body vibrates with this need for you. I leave without your touch. I drive home to my lover in San Francisco. We eat spaghetti sitting cross-legged on the floor of our unheated flat, our dinner plates balanced on upside down cardboard boxes.

Nightfall Exploration
Aviva Lilith

your eyes are planets.
with dark circles as asteroid belts, your freckles, comets
and each time an eyelash falls, it's a shooting star to wish upon.

the black hole of your mouth
entraps mine, as i am locked into this void. i never want to escape,
its a safely abstract dimension.

the galaxies clashing in your irises are unexplored.
but if it's the last thing i do,
i will navigate each rock and
ball of gas within them.

i am the only astronaut
in the universe of this sleeping girl,
and i am in search of every constellation.

This Poem Was Written to the Sound of Your Voice
Talia Rizzo

My grandmother asks if I am in love over the telephone of my car
as we drive through Utah,   tumbleweeds intertwining with tires.

The crunch of the highway. The fat mountains of salt.
Your hands warming beneath the mouth of my pants.

Who has the time to fall in love?

No one laughs. In July, I call for her birthday. She asks again. I talk
about golf, the humidity here. You come into the room from a
shower, towel dropping

at the door. At work, one of the chefs follows me into the walk-in
freezer sweat melting, goosebumps coating our arms, the buzz of the
cold. I pretend

to look for the lemon box. I know it is under the bin of red peppers.
I can't hear it,   but I know the other chefs are snickering,   eyebrows
raised.

/ *Why you always taking food home? You got*
a boyfriend?

His words are a breath of white smoke. I stick my finger deep into
The heart of an orange. The smell of dried chicken wings and sausage
behind me.

At the dentist on Miller Ave., the woman who sticks a metal pick
between my gums and asks "Bubblegum Or Mint?" is feeling chatty,

/ *My husband is from the Mid-West. He has*
such strong family values. I'm sure your man
does. They all do.

SMITTEN

I don't have a man, but my father is from Chicago.

/ Your father told me you met a boyfriend at college.
From the Mid-West. I ran into him at Molly Stone's.

In the seat three down from me, a man is having his teeth drilled into. Three cavities. Outside—the trees vibrate. His fists clench. I imagine that his eyes are closed.

I have some friends from Minnesota and Wisconsin.

She tells me I can't eat or drink anything for an hour. My mouth feels like a clump of newspaper shredding has been glued to my teeth. She winks at me as I leave. When

I arrive home, I find you draped over my childhood bed as if you were an extra sheet. Your bare body splayed out, sun ling your chest in zebra

stripes. Your shallow breath. The red arches of your sunburned breasts, the thick of your jutted hips. Splotched underwear. A car goes into panic

outside our window.

The Well of Loneliness

Sean Heather K. McGraw

Friends
I always thought
That I was prone to losing them right
After I came out or
At some point along the journey

(But growing up, everyone knew who I would be.)

Since
My church saw
Only condemnation of our love
It promised to me a
Life of holy celibacy.

(Because we don't deserve to be happy.)

Dark
Loneliness
To feel that unloved by every soul
That they demand my pain
-- suffering – and call it just reward

(Only they deserve happiness and love.)

Well
When she wrote
The Well of Loneliness, Radclyffe Hall,
She knew we all would crash
Why do people hurt the Other ones?

(One group defines itself by hatred for the outsider.)

I
Never felt more

SMITTEN

Truth in her plea for mercy, for love.
Humans tend to harm those
already burdened and blame them-

(As if all people get exactly what they deserve.)

Our
pain evidence
to them that we did wrong and deserve
punishment, and anguish.
Didn't Christ say of the blind man that

(Christ, do you love me?)

He
Did not sin,
Nor his parents, but that his healing
Would show the great glory
Of God, and even the woman

(Can I be healed?)

Who
Sinned was not
Condemned and their hypocrisy was
Known to all for they were
Greater sinners for their judgement.

(How ironic to be condemned for my love for her.)

When
I look at
Her face my joy is all unbounded.
In daytime and nighttime
Her face shines from the well's water.

(Can you try to feel as I feel?)

Scream
My heart screams
Radclyffe. Don’t drown, we will save you now.
Reach out your hands to mine.
Light beams sparkles on the water.

(In our embrace are we healed.)

What He Gave Away

Jennifer Mathews

When I was a child
my grandfather
gave us bruised apples and pears, stale bread.

They were throwing these away
he huffed, his affection delivered
in brown paper bags, aging
fruit I could smell
from the living room.

It's the 1990s, and now I live
in a different state, almost
500 miles from the scent
of my family. Four years
since
I've been told not to visit,
four years since I've made a life
with the woman I love.
And I finally show up
at their house
without calling.

Puckered by time
my grandparents sit
on summer porch chairs.
I walk up the front steps,
Grandpa Paul squints
and strains. Who's this, Annie?
It's me, I say.
He dashes into the house
to put in his teeth.

He invites me in
pours generic orange juice

puts applesauce, cheese and
chocolates down, saying Annie,
for godssake, get her some tea.
Full from lunch, I eat anyway. He rants
about President Clinton, property taxes
those lazy sons-of-bitches on welfare.
The yard looks nice, I say.

My grandmother winks at me
as I impress him with projects
my girlfriend has done, claiming
I painted the kitchen,
I found antique milk crates,
I refinished a dresser.
Taking credit just so I can talk
about my life.

I get ready to leave
and my grandpa
loads my car with
pots of wilting flowers
he got for next to nothing
until the trunk can barely close.
I take whatever he gives –
mums, geraniums, petunias.
He comments on my Honda
and those Japanese bastards.
I am back in the family.

Thanks, stupid heart
Jessica Jacobs

like for that time I'd banished her
number from every device I owned
only to find the digits scrawled on your
anterior wall. Diastole, you whispered,
relax and fill. But what did you know?
Flushing and pumping like a jellyfish
going nowhere, stuffed between my lungs
pink wings like a flightless bird, ugly.
The trick pony of my brain was ready
to wander other pastures, wonder other
futures, but you—grown from the same stock
as courage and accord—she was your only
aim, and faithful dumb muscle you are, stupid
beautiful heart, you beat only for her.

Watching, To Know Love
Sarah Bigham

An errant hit, ball meets spectator's
skull -- muscled arms whisk slack
ones from bleachers to Mustang
to ER. Strength and speed seem
musts. Rings wound with twine to
fit smaller fingers as larger hands
turn angry. Passion trumps caution.
Overnight traveler missing a partner
to pack the suitcases and anticipate a
return. Spouse as helpmate and
companion. What to wait for, and to
wish for. Butterhead among chicory.
Safety amidst chaos.
Tenderness does abide.

Originally published in *Minnie's Diary*

Ode to Provincetown

Carol H. Jewell

From Commercial Street, I can see
the Pilgrim Monument, topped by its
"Donald Duck" visage,
seagoing boats,
tourists looking for whales,
an unnamed beach at low tide
with a cantering horse and rider, bareback,
the public library—built in 1860,
competing stands of salt water taffy,
pretty boys, bears, and fairies,
snowqueens, dykes, and femmes,
tweeners and giddy teens,
posters: GET TESTED. BE SAFE. NO SMOKING.
your green eyes, smiling at me.

Every Minute of Us
Izabell Jöraas Skoogh

It is 3:07 AM
thoughts slowly approaching my mind,
like the elf's tiptoeing around Santa Claus on Christmas Day,
not to wake him up.
It is 3.11AM
and the thoughts are now reaching the corner of my mind
expanding my mind, with all these possible outcomes
for all these different scenarios.
It is 3:15 AM
my head is pounding,
it is such a tremendous ache.
Almost competing with the ache
I feel in my chest.
3:17 AM
and I think about all the people in her life,
that one point in time loved her.
3:27 AM
I think about those people who loved her for the wrong reasons,
loved her wrongfully.
3:37 AM
I think about all the people in my life,
that one point in time loved me.
3:39 AM
I think about those who loved me for the wrong reasons,
loved me wrongfully.
3:40 AM
Then I think about it more closely.
What if my love is the right love for her because it is for the right reason.
and what if her love is the right one for me because it is for the right
reason.
3:59 AM
I think of her.

Perceptions of You

Ruth Bowley

Time is not relevant when I am with you.

As though,
a morning's rush...
Had taken both my shoes.
Unusual or not...
I tread so lightly on the air.
Barefoot or not...

I hold tightly to the image of your cares.

And, the day...

Never set anew without my recollections of you.

So, often, I speak to the dawn.
'What is it I should do?'
How do I navigate the perceptions of you.

Yet,
it is like asking the night's rain of the morning's dew.

Fever
Tia M. Hudson

On the phone last night
She asked if I suffer from spring fever
and hinted at desire
stroked my breast with her voice,
matched my heart's beat with her breathing.
Oh, today spring fever is all I can think about
I cry for cool water, soft breezes.

Silhouettes
Alison Palmer

Here are a hundred tools.
Here, where I toil, I think about
                    remembering you again.
*
Yesterday, winter wind at the side of
your face.
          It takes courage to bother with
the entirety of beauty—
I watched your cheek grow pink.
I thought about touching it with a single
          finger, perhaps mistaken for
more wind.
*
And the sum of our parts beg only
                    for more parts...
The motion of us together is not greater than
the emotion of the future:
us
is merely another tool you present
          me with, promise of forever-memory, yet
what I believe in are sad letters.
*
Yesterday was simple; we walked unnoticed
through a park. This, you told me,
          is where the sides of things come
to die. Hand in hand, what I heard you say was, We
                    can be more than what renders
the whole. Here, we build,
we remember each other with the frequency of lovers.

After the burning
Carla Toney

In the forest
below the falls
like my heart
after the burning,
charred stumps of spruce,
scarred birch and aspen,
pine boughs scattered like
dismembered skeletons.

I thought life would never
come again - no seed could
survive such devastation,
but fireweed carried on the wind,
eats into the black soot of earth,
takes root in charred rock and
in the spring on the wind I see
purple heads of fireweed dancing

And you,
my love,
after the fire,
after the burning,
have taken root
in the ash of my soul
and wax there,
my fireweed.

This is who I am
C. E. Wing

This is who I am
No apologies
No excuses
I am a woman
I may dress and appear masculine
This is who I am
I don’t want to be a man
I love feminine women
But I am a woman
And I am a stud
This is who I am
There are others like me

And there are some that do feel they are male

But I am a woman
I support and stand by them
Because this is who I am
Love is love
We are stronger together
I am a woman
And I feel no shame
This is who I am

This Splendid Sunrise

Henri Bensussen

You have no idea how it is
for a woman who's not a bottle
of port. Aging isn't going well.
Take this splendid sunrise—
imagine me ten years ago
when I was somewhat beautiful
Chromatic notes have faded
to the scale of gray, forfeiture
of brightness in every cell
Except a few up in the brain
the ones that can't remember
how old they are. Like that bell
That got Pavlov's dog to salivate
I rise to an intensity of longing
in the presence of a tall, sexual
Butch pristinely starched
pledged to sisterly friendship
she says, not the sort of wild
sunrise I ardently desire, still.

If Only I'd Been Brave Enough

Kim D. Bailey

Regret sits like a cat
on my chest, digging
purring with my disillusionment of her kiss, her lips
a swing, pushing until the new
heights hold me
hostage,
and I hold
my breath comes
in shallow graves of dead
children's dreams, there is no
place for this love.
Bravery is broken ladders
leaning against warped wood, overgrown
with weeds covered
with rust.

Meet me on a Sunless Day
Nayana Nair

the sun is so much brighter than it used to be.
it makes me wonder if I remember my days correctly.
has it always been like this?
or have my eyes created their own darkness.
(is there a word for it?
like there is a word for plants creating food from the drops of sun)
were you always this beautiful?
were you always looking at me with those kind eyes?
my broken mind only remembers cruel gazes.
why did it never take your image in?
how is it so easy to not see?
why is it so easy to believe the worst?
what if I walk over to you, try to smile with you,
and call what I feel love?
how long will my new vision stay with me?
do you know how to love a blind bitter person?
I am asking since I am always not like this.
I am asking because I want to meet you again on a dark cloudy day.
I want you to know of my blindness
before you love me back.

First Pomegranate
Alison Stone

Which part of this crimson
honeycomb to eat? And how? Sun
highlights the knife's blade, stripes the room
like prison bars.
I watch you scoop seeds, then copy;
savor sweet-tart bursts
as red pearls open.

Your food soothes me, your kind,
scratched-by-smoke-and-whiskey voice.
You must meditate, Sweet Pea.
Learn to let go. You're just like me
at that age – beautiful and charming,
far too stubborn.
Not with you.
I read the Trungpa books
you lend me, obey
traffic signs, take vitamins.
Juice stains your lips.
Suddenly clumsy, I spill
water, lose my spoon in the shag
rug. I've had offers, always thought
I didn't fancy women.
Your blond hair.
Your breasts.
No one is that heterosexual.
Now I understand why my ex-boyfriend
sucked a chain of bruises down my neck
the first time I said yes.
Not passion, possession.
"Friend" is a pallid word.
Mentor, motherish though not kin,
I have no way
to mark you mine.

This Is What Loves Looks Like

This jaundiced light's
too bright. It slices
my hand as I dig in the devoured
pomegranate's rind for hidden seeds.
Your husband
due back soon.
Your voice, your hair.
My hunger.

Eyes Shut Open
Marvlyn Vincent

They say love is blind,
that it's an emotion,
and will take over your mind.
But at the same time
they question who you love
using words from the Bible
saying that it is a displeasure to the one above.
The same one who created love
attribute in your existence
the reason you live
the meaning of feelings
questioning what is.
We're giving a gift, handed to us
that we might freely give
with no conditions and no remorse.
Yet there are those who just can't help it.
They're standing here judging
attaching your emotion and feeling
to sinning not healing
or real meaning.
Behind this life, that we're living
to them you must say,
your judgments are unwarranted.
you sit back glaring,
hiding behind eyes that make those people feel like they're hunted
and on this Earth
they're not welcomed, they're not wanted.
Now put yourself in their shoes
picture of the one above,
if you were he
who would you choose
the one not preaching just words but doing his dues
other one so caught up
judging what's right from wrong

that they only true expression of Love
is what's heard in a song.

the box, cross-hatched, my knees

after Richard Siken's Litany in Which Certain Things Are Crossed Out

Mandy Grathwohl

Tonight, Anne, I beg you: be my God.
The pinot noir can be the Ghost
and me the Son, your humble baby.
You'll touch me, frantic, your fingers cold and wet
from the dishes now drying,
frozen in time and in love with your gentle grasp.
Won't you call me sick and wrap me
in your blanket, red with womanness? Won't you
take me in your car and show me wonders,
drive through the puddles and laugh
as the ducks go flying?
I was born a bad seed,
choking on this life. I came out silent
and tore through my mother. My hair was so black
my father smelled smoke.
I was not meant for smallness, Anne,
and sadness swallows me.
It unhinges its jaw and it devours me.
Take me to your favorite boutique
and tell me about the dream you had
about the car crash and the rabbit
and how it meant something.
Tell me about the garage.
Tell me about your daughter
and how you loved her.
Tell me about my mother, Anne.
Tell me what her hair looks like.
Tell me if she weeps for me.
Drive me to her house and paint its fence with me
and scold me when I drop the paintbrush.
Touch me with your clammy hands, your ring gone,
the dishwater smell inside you.

This Is What Loves Looks Like

Tell me sorry and swipe my hair away.
Look at me with your blue eyes and tell me about the arctic.
Tell me where I came from.
Tell me that my black hair was a blessing
and my silence predicted happiness.
Tell me that your hands are dry.
Tell me that God greeted you as you drove past Heaven
and that he clambered into your Oldsmobile
and tell me what you talked about.
Tell me His hair was wild and that He sounded like windchimes.
Tell me that you drove all night
and felt something in the morning.
Tell me that crying makes miracles.
Tell me that the milk I drank made my bones strong.
Tell me that the towers had to fall and that children have to die.
Tell me that everything beautiful is waiting patiently for me,
but the sink is full, and your hands are dirty,
and someone is calling your name.

Embrace
Tre L. Loadholt

you pull me into you,
breaths panting,
the air of our home--a solid force
for ripe intimacy,
I sink...
the battle of loving you
is one I'll fight forever
and ever if
I get to savor
the nectar dripping from your lips
as long as we both shall
live.

Wild things
Jesica Nodarse

And I'd normally say
"Don't love a wild one, like me"
But she...
She's the wild... incarnate
Belonging is the chaos in her chest

Love 1
SATU

To love her
Jesica Nodarse

What is it like to be loved by her?
It is like the wild pulling you in for a tight hug
It is like the ocean letting you dive in for as long as you want, and your lungs never giving up
It is a sunset that never ends
It is a storm that rages on around you but keeps you safe nestled within
It's madness that makes perfect sense
It is magic
It is intense to the point of sweet pain
Best of all...
Loving her is like coming home, all the lights are on
And you know...
That inside is everything that you have been waiting for

Blue Was Not the Warmest Color

Christine E. Ray

our parting was not such sweet sorrow
it was piercing pain
sleepless nights
wrenching sobs
Melissa Etheridge played
on endless loop
no comfort to be found
lover & best friend both lost
in a stunningly abrupt
goodbye

blue was not the warmest color
as you packed our past
and your jeans
in your suitcase
before walking casually out our door
her car waiting at the curb
We can still be friends
your parting words

I don't want to be friends
I want to be the ghost
that never lets you rest
the name it always hurts to say
the one you regret the rest of your
damn long life
because this pain has your
name all over it
the parting gift I never asked for
and would like to return to sender

Dream Interpretation

Kelsey Hontz

Junior year of high school, wearing a low ponytail and lower self-esteem,
I open my dream dictionary, run my finger down the entries, past "set (chess)" and "set (table)"
Until the three-letter word that jumps like ants onto my psyche:
"Sex" sits boldly there, right on the middle of the page, and anyone in this classroom could just
Lean right over and watch me discover the secrets of the universe.
Because without the book, I can't make sense of this puzzle,
Why I should have these dreams about
Not TJ, tall with seafoam eyes, or Tyler, football-team-scented, or Jessie and his guitar but
About Katie, about Beth, always piled onto me like
The softest pillows of flesh,
Calling my name, holding it in their teeth like a pearl of sugar, melting over and over
In my hands.
The dream dictionary suggests that to dream about sex means
You need to work something out with the person,
But I have never even spoken to them, aside from once
Complimenting two beautiful Friday dresses, my words tumbling
Out of my braces like yesterday's food scraps, spoiled as soon as they touched the air.
What did we need to work out in low-lit rooms, red and red and pink
Rolling like waves, shuddering, wetness?
The dream dictionary also suggests that there is attraction to acknowledge.
I tell it no, I remind it, myself, of TJ, Tyler, Jessie and his guitar
I flip the pages, fan of a madwoman, but those are the only suggestions,
And the entry for "normal"
Doesn't sound like me at all.

Patching the walls of my apartment I wish you well

Piper Michelle

Young spider,
I hope someone
falls into your web
so that we both may eat.
You and Mars are my closest friends
watching me
through the half-shut window
as I carefully avoid sleep,
you and the turmeric nail polish
I tease my toes with,
and the two cartons of vanilla rice milk
I inherited from my friend
who is not dying
but moving to Kentucky
which may be the same thing.
Her partner is going with her
if they were the only two people in heaven
I'd be happy.
I'm filling wagons to pilgrimage
five blocks away
kicking my heels to a bullfrog-green
squat cave where I'll kiss
the light-switches goodnight.
I'm jealous,
young spider,
you have mars, and turmeric nail polish
flirts with my toes;
the cartons of rice milk are married
and my friends are the happiest ghosts I know.
Set me up.
I want my lover to be exciting—running yolk, snap pea, grape popsicle
I want to eat.

Fields, Early June, A Love Song

Rachael Ikins

Timothy-grass is everywhere.
Shoulder-High,
nodding gray-fringed
green lashes, it whispers
secrets to the west wind.
Looks me in the eye.

Yellow mustard patches
sneezed into pockets of field.
Stain the hillside, neon intensity.

Wild oats dangle their earrings
against Earth's neck.

Dusk, light against dark velvet,
cornfield as I drive down rt 20
through the valley.

You bow your head over the hoe.
Broad shoulders stroke tilled rows
between tomatoes and broccoli and hills
of squash.

A dove practices his flute from forest edge.
Your hair blends with timothy colors.
My heart sings its quiet song. Fields,
early June.

Nantucket
Katharine Love

darling:
long have i waited
breath by breath
for your arrival.
i must be
honest my love
there were times
(days//months//years)
when i thought you
would never appear,
yet you are here
fully embodied,
complete and whole.
the totality of
your love
forces me to acknowledge
(slowly, ever so slowly)
that i am deserving of kindness
and a place in this world.
i love getting lost
in the deep of you
feeling joined in a way
i've never felt before –
my own unified theory.
memories of Nantucket
the winter
of our content
searching for sea glass
on the frozen sand
your sturdy arms always
protecting me
from the cool wind
that blew the sand
into our eyes, and mouth

and hair.
i remember
how we ran
together
into a cove,
seeking shelter
from a
sudden snowstorm.

i kissed the nape
of your neck,
your skin oh your skin,
tasting as sweet
as maple syrup
drizzled on vanilla ice cream.
something shifted for me
on that windswept beach
in Nantucket
in the deep recesses
of the cove.
despite the dampness
of the wet sand
i felt a warmth
infuse my body,
a knowing that
you will be
here
a heart without
question
someone to watch over me.

Willowy Rose & Chrysanthemum

Lynne Burnett

At a table, over wine, two women
bent their heads toward each other
(willowy rose and chrysanthemum),
hushed words drifting down
upon two hands entwined
above the gift of a ring,
as steadily they leaned
into the garden
that chose them,
young stems glorying
in the bud of a caress, full bloom
of love upon their faces, and we,
a table of husbands and wives,
were as helpless as them
to turn our heads away
from such a graceful rain of light,
so firm a reach of roots
across forbidden ground.

For Alice, Summer 2005

Jamie L. Smith

Champs Elysees smells like happiness—
high jasmine notes riding freesia and amber, with
hints of guilt. Like sleeping in this one last
summer day—warm, rose scented light,
waking you into morning.

See, this is how I love you—
by shuffling around barefoot in the pale
square of five-am light my window lets in,
wrapping hands around my red coffee cup,
with its hairline crack, palms pressing against
heat. Then I glance at my bed sheets—rumpled
without you, now so foreign to me.

I hope you'll wake up this morning
in an inhale of perfume from the pillow next to you.
A few strands of gold—all you'll find in my place,
you'll spin them in your fingers, then slip
your ring back on.

Palette
Kai Coggin

last night before sleep
she drew pictures on my back with her fingers
a test of my spacial recognition my ability to form
a horse a sun
a sailboat
from the movement of her fingertip traces against my skin
to see it
take shape in my mind's eye invisible palette

the curvature of my back competing with her delicate design of
flower
fish smile
and I cannot guess
cannot translate the trace to shape each time   she erases
whole palm swipes in the dark tries again

rabb
it
snail
and I am the worst at this game because
just being touched
by the fingertip of this artist
just having my skin rise   to meet her

all I can picture in these traces is

Heaven Heaven Heaven
a reddening flame

the wall of who she thinks she has to be crumbles

into

p
e
t
a
l
s

and becomes a narrow path toward her a path I walk becoming
aperture
lens glass focusing on the destination that is her the journey of our
mutual creation
our hearts
speaking to each other
and listening at the same time

Halfway/Passages

Rachael Ikins

Cut my curls,
spike the remnants high.
Pull off my bra.
Let other hair grow.
Shove my hands into
baggy cargo pockets.
Cultivate a bad-ass saunter.
Delicious, dangerous dyke, curious,
open your cupboards wide.
To wash your shoulders,
rinse fragrant water down your laddered spine.
To bushel your moon-pale breasts
In my elbows' amorous crook.
Midnight,
Candlelight.
When you recline
among your pink pillows,
one hand behind your head.
Like a Reubens nude.
Floor creaks.
You smile, no doubt.
Door hinges squeak.
I come out.

When I Photograph a Woman
Kai Coggin

that moment
when I photograph a woman a woman I hardly know
and she begins to bend to me
a tulip s t r e t c h i n g for a spot in sunlight she lets
stiffness and fear
fall to the
floor
(a silk dress)

her muscles relax
under my glassy gaze it takes time *sure*
it takes both of us being a little scared

but there is always the sudden turn where her cheek
becomes more of a song
where her shoulders and confused hands become a stillness
strong assured rest
where her eyes
become a soft glimmer invitation and she lets me in
a door opens to her hallowed shrine and
I find
her vulnerable story lens flaring
at her light

a wildflower bursting from hillside a quiet moon rising glow
a moving ocean

They said our love was not real
Alicia Sophia

They said our love wasn't real
That I was confused
That it was just a phase
Something I would grow out of
They said our love was against nature
That it wasn't real
But they didn't know that when I laid in your arms and kissed your lips, it felt more real than the ground I'm standing on
Being with you never felt wrong
But I greet their frowns and stares with a smile, I crumble their hate notes, while I throw it back to them as I pull you closer and keep loving you

The Nature of Shame

Angie Waters

Madder Root

Didi Artier

You said use madder root it will
bring out the highlights in your hair.
Will you touch me if I do? Will you
stop looking at boys and turn your attention
to the girl who sits in the sun trying to reflect
a little of your glory back at you?
We sit with our feet touching, your toes
are smaller than mine and dig into the sand
like hot crabs.
I want to lean over and take your hand,
curl it like a shell and place it over my heart
but everyone would look and point
at two teenage lesbians on the beach.
Instead, I write about you in my diary
and everything I write, is hoping you will
betray my trust and read
the reasons I bled roses
for you
at 17.

Dusk
Erin King

Moonlight
Silvers our lips and lashes
You and I skinny-dipping
On tippy-toes
Hair clinging wet
To our shoulders
Fingers moving in arcs
trailing bubbles behind.

Currents pulling below
As lake-wet kisses begin
And the pines rise darkly above
The still water.

Bravery is doing it anyway
Avital Abraham

I'm afraid of celery
because I think it's too stringy,
and too easy to choke on.
I'm afraid of throwing up in public,
and throwing up in general.
I'm afraid of spiders,
spiders and specks of dust on the ceiling that
look like spiders but aren't actually spiders.
I'm afraid of planning for the future
because what if things don't work out.
I'm afraid of not planning for the future
mostly because of the same reason.
I'm afraid of the unseen things that
lurk downstairs after I turn the lights off.
They cannot be seen or heard
but instead felt somewhere deep in my stomach.
I'm afraid of going to the dentist by myself,
and getting shots,
flying on airplanes,
and reading my poetry,
which is not to say I don't do these things,
I do,
they just scare me.
I'm afraid of getting things out of the toaster oven,
because burns hurt for long after you
actually made contact with the thing
you shouldn't have.
I'm afraid of change,
and falling in love,
and breaking my heart,
or breaking someone else's.
So that's maybe why right now,
more than anything,
I'm really afraid of you

What She Loves
Jennifer Mathews

She is not
supposed to lie
on asphalt in summer rain
wearing white. Or roll down

the muddy banks like a child
arms to her sides
giving herself to gravity.

She's not supposed to cherish
jumping spiders, or turning
the compost, or the stench

of stagnant beaver ponds.
She is not supposed to love the wrinkles
etching the edges of a woman's

eyes or the taste of clean sweat
on her lover's shoulder
after they've spent the morning

weeding the garden. Still, she loves
what she loves. Like standing over
a hot stove, boiling down blueberries

on a humid afternoon, and
twirling gracelessly, until dizziness spins her
into the grass.

It would be so easy to love you
Rebecca Sanchez

Guide me to the nape,
the cavity beyond these roaming
hills. I won't say a word to your flared
jeans and muffled shoe laces, shuffling
clumps of dirt between your soles,
barley tickling your scalp, your snapback
clawing the current. Your snapback wobbling
like wildflowers, spewing nectar. You reach
for my hand and I give you my heart.

(whisper)
I ache to unearth your tangled roots,
my fists wringing your dewy residue
into the palm of my hand.

Our backbones crunch bark as
sharp bristles of spruce splinter
my cheek, an unlit Camel cigarette
suspended between the breach
of your lips like dandelion.
Your jaw quivers, knuckles
rummaging frayed pockets, fruitless
and you curse, biting your tongue.
I sway beneath your shadow.
I know you would set yourself aflame
if only you could find your missing
lighter.

Your freckles graze specks of sunlight
and once again I am   stumbling
over my own two feet.
I know these rivers are humbled
by the murmur of your footsteps.
And your kisses,

like the caress of juniper.

Your limbs shuffle along these rugged
plains and I swear   I can hear your name
in the weeping of the willows, goosebumps
slithering along the aged husk and broad
blades. I swear I can feel your pulse
in the sting of zephyr upon my cheeks
and yet this loneliness is
a splinter imbedded in my palm
and the rush of rainwater over my ankles.
I cannot rid my skin of your
touch.
I'm not sure
I want to

And When Did It Begin?
Wandeka Gayle

Was it when you rolled your r's and recreated the Puerto Rico of your childhood, meshing with my Jamaican water spirits and ancestral soothsayers?

Was this bond inevitable, island girls traversing the New Mexico mountains in search of our voices?

Was it when I first saw you and I, buckled in place beside you so high over those mountains, listened as you spoke to me like we had met long before time?

Was it just then, when you tucked a stubborn curl behind your ear and your smile, caramel and fluid, held me there, stealing the breath from me?

Was it when you tried to teach me merengue while cast in the neon orange glow, something else besides the thumping bass pulsing through me?

Was it your arms tight around my waist that lingered a beat longer, when we had to say goodbye?

Was it the effervescent kisses you sprinkled across each cheek when I saw you again and you smelled like sweet fruit and danger?

Was it your softness melding itself to mine in that embrace, making me ache to reach down and taste you?

Was it when I open my eyes now, years since and still find you there hovering, fully formed, graceful, too perfect for this world?
Just when did it begin?

When was it that your essence seeped into my blood, pooling through my being, awakening something so potent and persistent?

I don't know, love.

I only know I want to be enveloped in it, no longer silent, no longer questioning, no longer afraid.

Imprisonment
Shraddhanvita Tiwari

the diamond ring
stays on the finger

the red *tikka*
crowns the brows

framed photographs
rest on the barren walls

purple bruises
hide behind the curls

the measures the space
between body and soul

big charcoal eyes
envelop a distant face

the room imprisons
her flesh and bones

her spirit flies
to the land unknown

You are what takes my breath away
Emily Alice DeCicco

No matter the backdrop,
no matter how beautiful
the beaches
the canyons
the ruins,
I'll turn back to you.
You are what takes my breath
and sends chills down my spine.
You are my only undoing.

Woman
Hoda Abdulqadir Essa

The altar
A swaying heart beat
Coils up to heaven's crescent
With a smile rivaling the sun.
You smolder
And I cannot help but fan the flames.
You gift me a gourd
Watering holes
One that overflows
& unfurls a vision
Another set of eyes in me.
Eyes that see beyond
What sight can see.
You give me magma
Hot as lava
Sweet as honey
And pour it seamlessly
Into my lap.
You gift me a flame
One that washes me clean
Purifies me
Washing away remnants
All the small filaments
Filling us with an orange hum
Crackling like Fire
Electricity washing over
And you teach me
The ways to live in a body
That has the nerve to be
This free.

Bathing in St. Petersburg
Rebecca Ruth Gould

I scrubbed your back &
rubbed you with birch branches
until your skin shed
layers on my hands.
We bathed each other.
The sulfur scorched us clean as newborn babes.
Even then, my friend,
distance intervened between us.
We touched with the tender touch
of strangers who will never meet again
but who recognize in each other's
hands a fleeting epiphany.

Room 415
Olivia Chachinsky

I want to spend my heaven
with you on the fourth floor
of the seedy hotel where we first met.
Its neon sign cuts the blue-black
night with slices of orange—sharp and sweet.
I'd like to hold you close to my heaving
chest, wrapping my arms around your waist
and feeling rather than seeing
your arm move as you brush your teeth.
Before we know it, the stained carpet will open
beneath us, and we will fall into that dark womb
feet first, clinging onto each other for dear life. I will rip
your skin with my long nails and you will bite
my lip until all we taste is rich, red blood and rust
and kerosene. You, my love, will burn like Joan of Arc,
screaming when your body bursts into inevitable flames.
Ava, I have no answers to the questions I have asked;
I have not prayed to a God that responds
or to a man who could ever understand
the words flowing from my aching mouth.
I have not tossed runes from a velvet pouch
to know the meaning of an unforgiving life,
nor have I looked for signs in the cracked carcasses
beside the road, but I know that as I lay dying,
I will love everything you are and all
you cannot be. I will find you as beautiful
as I did that night when the stars rained white fire
above our heads. When my flesh is gone, when my heart
is gone, my love for you will still remain,
red and tender and beating next to you in the darkness of room 415.

so she's a wound
Cassandra Bumford

i could tell you her name,
but all you need to know is
she was a pistol.
she didn't mean to shoot me.
sometimes the war she fought
inside caused her to fire at
unsuspecting passersby.
she took great care in tending
to my wounds, humming
hallelujah to calm the pain of
her, wedging between my ribs,
shared her drinks with me so we
could swap lipstick without ever
actually kissing.
i was not her only casualty,
and she was not the only one at war.
now i'm left with bullets inside me.
she never said to remove them.
i've found it is hard to breathe
while she's hiding inside me.

Again

M. Duckett-Ireland

I took a second shower for you today
even though I figured you wouldn't come.
The towel. Still damp from this morning—
but only
in the spots that hadn't let go
of earlier.
The most saturated.
Its passage against my cheek
sent me climbing into a wet one-piece
on vacation with my family
when I was young. I would
struggle
to get the suit up,
the cold of yesterday's sea water
slicing through my lines of pink burn
into every nerve beneath.
My body would draw back,
not wanting all that sensation at once
but so wanting what would follow.
And that
that reminded me of you.

Previously published on the *Negative Culpability Press Website.*

A Wolf

Rachel Winter Roth

It can only be felt in the bright of a pure black night
The absence of life and death, otherwise known as eternity
Tonight, every night, it'll stretch to meet the horizon in a clean smooth line
Scattered across the line are the loons who breathe in the night of a full moon
Its light breathes lust
So strong we might combust
Under its light our bones crack and blood will flood our mouths
Two legs become four and now there's nothing we can't outrun
Behind us, you might find a fleshless mound of hollow skin lying where we once stood
A new skin for a new beginning that'll only last the night
We bred with the Earth
Now we have some girth
A hundred cries of seclusion crying out in union
Such haunting cries might have driven us mad, if they weren't such a comfort
Tonight, every night, we live wild and free
Or perhaps that's the lie we rehearse as the sun's yellow head sneaks its way up the horizon
We cry to our Mother
But never feel her smother
It's a shame all we get is our Father, marching beside his massive hordes
We are pillagers, he says, the night is the best time of our lives
The saying sounds familiar, but it's from a life long ago
Two in one, we're lost in a form where we run faster than ever before
I'm not a werewolf
I'm nothing but a wolf

Dear Doubleslutoreo

Teresa T. Chappell

I would call you a bad influence,
except that you're not. Maybe I
don't understand the thrill you
get when you hang out the window
to light a bowl, or the way you enjoy alcohol
burning down your throat. But I do know
you will answer on the first ring
& cook me dinner when my head
is muffled & my body aches. You're
always late, but I know you'll show
up. We've taken to calling each other
sisters—created a shared way of being.
Let it stand, here today, that I will gladly
open the creases of my palms & let
my blood mingle with yours

Random Girl No More
Dr. Sneha Rooh

And lemongrass.
Like life force
Like hurricane in the heart
Like the strength of the hold right in the middle of the kiss.
Like floating on water
Like a lucid dream
Like sunshine on bare back
You taste like a sigh
Like recognition
Like the saltiness of a magnet
Like a back rub
Like two lovers playing magic fingers
And the static electricity between.
You taste like patience.
Like the tree that has seen many seasons
You taste like a tear drop
One that is astonished to flow during joy
Like the flame of an oil lamp
Like reflection on water
You taste like eye contact.

If you want to write a love poem
Carol H. Jewell

you must include:
the night we fell asleep inside each other,
velvet and warm,
pink petals spread across pillows,
you feeding me briny olives, one by one,
a vanilla-scented candle,
fuchsite eyes,
Chrissie Hynde on the small stereo,
"The Lottery," by Shirley Jackson,
your downy skin,
finally reaching the itch in the small of my back.

A Love Letter Too Embarrassing to Read

A. Lawler

You don't know me well.
I have told you all there is to tell,
But the words are a chalk outline,
And I have been gone a very long time.
But let's go back to that bar
Where we found that spark
And I can tell you everything all over again.
This time I'll do whatever you say because I need you as more than a friend.
You want something casual? Ask away.
I'll give you anything you like to make you stay.
I gave you more of myself than I know how to live without.
I'll give you the rest, every inch of me is yours now.
Follow me to the bar and we can start over again.
Remind me how to breathe
With your hands all over me.

Soft mouth
Selene Crosier

I wasn't ready
maybe that's what attracted me to you
treasured and worthless
your invert chest
the ribs of a child
pluck a chord
sing a tune
I own
nothing but one
moment
watching you swim naked
the search of sound
pines still holding their grudge
your eyes emptied
your lips broken against wait
against my still entreaty
I trust nothing
only the jig of life
in your gamine limbs
spelling out the position of
dropped clothes like constellations
curtseys before the heavy curtain

comes down on our budding ardor
I feel old
against your new
shine
I feel young
against your ancient
eyes
I trust no-one except
the first sound
flickering over your face
as I dive

through
as sleek as a silver fern
shedding its urge
making magic of forest floor
all the glittering wonderment
in your soft mouth

True Love
Alexandra Short

You still love her, because
Love doesn't dissolve like a soft candy
Meeting the warmth of your tongue.
Love doesn't just disappear like a magic trick.
Love transforms like ice turns to water.
True love is linear and infinite.

Sappho

Alexandria Moore

She collects stones to mail
To her loved ones
One is a poet like me
We walk along a dried up river bank
Comb through pebbles
Later I give her one when she cries
Not out of softness but
Because I was laughing

You can't write about violets without being sapphic

This is not a love letter
I am violet-tressed but not violet-lapped
I will comb through fragments looking
For meaning
Looking for a smooth round stone that
Fits to the contours of my hand

The internet tells me I might be a biromantic heterosexual

We go out to dinner and it
Looks like a first date
Speak of all the people who broke
Our hearts
Laugh over red wine that
Stains plum not purple

People think of us as a pair
Joke that they feel like they're at
A lesbian dinner table and
When I ask her to make me tea
I know she will bring it to me by the window
It smells like strawberries

SMITTEN

The girl in my twelfth grade history class
Used to have strawberry colored hair
I sat next to her every day
Wanted her to like me
Properly
But not much else
Later I would describe it as a schoolgirl crush
But not much else

Why have I always wanted to lie with boys
When they make me cry about my womanhood
Why have I always wanted to lie with boys
When Sappho writes so beautifully of
The tenderness of falling asleep on your lover's breast
And the sweet taste of violets on your lips

My Heart Recognized Her Before I Did
Tan Shivers

The first time I saw her, our eyes locked,
and I instantly found myself lost in reverie
My soul drank from her cocoa brown
eyes like a desert wanderer upon the
discovery of water
Discerning my astonishment, she smiled
and proceeded to extend her right hand
towards mine
As her name rolled off of her lips, I
faintly heard my heart whisper, "It's her!"
Confused by its assertion, I slowly stretched
out my hand and uttered my name
The moment our hands touched, my mind suddenly
comprehended the two small, yet profound,
words my heart proclaimed just seconds earlier
My body slightly jolted at the electrifying touch
as it, too, now understood what my heart meant
It was her. The "her" I had never seen, yet
spent countless hours daydreaming about
The "her" for whom I was willing to give up a
life of promiscuity to fully pursue monogamy
The "her" I thought of whenever I listened to the
melodic sound of Max Richter's "Spring 1"
Our hands, still joined in the union of a hand
shake, exchanged secrets of an unforetold future
After what seemed like a brief eternity, our hands
unlocked, but our spirits remained intertwined
And now, I stood there before her, like a treasure seeker
who had unearthed the most priceless of findings
A once unfamiliar soul now became as familiar as my own.

Explosives
Aviva Lilith

not every explosion
contains plutonium.
californium
(Cf)
is also used.

explosions happen
when you tell
catholic parents you are a girl
dating a girl
(Pu).

californium
is used to help start up
nuclear
reactors.

californium
is the kiss before you
tell.

Blooming Kisses
Jennifer Carr

Sometimes her kisses
are soft like a ladybug
landing on a Calendula.
Other times her kisses
are hard like heavy rains
landing on the geraniums.
It doesn't matter the kind
of kisses she gives me
because on this earth
I am a flower planted
in the soil of her garden
Just waiting -
for the next opportunity
to bloom again.

For Natalie

after Danez Smith

Kay Shamblin

apricot nectar bruises the cheeses resting in our palms & baby
cats crawl on the front stoop & crush petals
until they bloom from the edges of your chapbook & drip
like the last drop of over sweetened coffee built in my hands
& enter a d&d session with tears
of laughter already staining our faces & foolish
longing ringing true with an arrow singing
in both of our chests & garden
daydreams with the sun still
climbing to reach its peak & hard-loved thrift store furniture
with cup rings sunken on every surface & i will keep putting you in
this poem
until it becomes a ballad & juice spiked with cheap vodka spills
from the sides of both of our mouths & kiss-printed cheeks &
a lesbian love song floats from the open windows & my hands hang
off the sides of your thighs & Natalie, I see your smile
in the edge of every magnolia leaf, every starling's wing & O, I
would drink
your grin if I could & poem about tenderness
until it hangs as sweet as a ripe peach & questions spark
our 1am debates & reach across tabletops
to rest my fingers on yours & summer's bittersweet arms
wrap around us & this is an ode to your too-small tank tops &
understanding eyes & vulgarities sounding sweet
on your tongue & wishes
pressed into fountain coins, eyelashes &
xenia for all our friends & your laugh
could resurrect this sleeping heart & zinnias
bloom - despite the season - in both of our hands

Katie Bouman and Other Unreachable Women

Kelsey Hontz

On the day the first ever photo of a black hole came out,
So did the one of you and your new girlfriend.
The last transmission from you in my inbox
Was "let me think about that"
Re: where you would take me on a date.
I think you felt it cosmically approaching;
I think it pulled you away from me,
Through to her.
I am grateful to it.
I have never really understood space
Even though I am half astronaut.
The space suits have never really fit me,
Never been small enough to be just my size.
I have always only explored the depths of the sea
That have been shallower and filled with more obstacles
Than pearls.
You and she are not like the black hole.
You are a rainbow, prismatic, filled with
More colors than our photographs can yet capture,
Than my eyes can capture,
Sitting in my wet-suit in some unplumbed darkness
Wondering why I did not shine for you.

Worship
Carrie Lee Connel

Black silk scarf brushed with cerulean blue,
wrapped about the head like a turban,
covers your strawberry blonde tresses.
Earlobes left exposed to reveal
four-inch ankhs hanging down;
made of balsa wood, the weight together
not more than the feather Anubis
measures against the Pharaoh's heart.
I wonder why you sit here in a wooden pew
instead of kneeling on the ground
beneath a canopy of branches –
oak, maple and yew speaking in tongues
only the wind understands.
You wear a cotton tunic and flowing skirt to the ankles.
With your waist-length hair loose,
you should be sky-clad
in front of the Goddess,
lighting candles at the four directions,
invoking the elements.
Evocative of the Pre-Raphaelite ideal:
a mid-19th Century spinster sister
living to her own doctrine;
heavy-lidded eyes reminiscent
of Lizzie Siddal's self-portrait, painted
if she had lived a decade longer.

First published in *Synaeresis,* Issue 7, Harmonia Press, 2019

Deviant Bent
Susi Bocks

I don't know what you like
you don't know what I like
The head thinks it's normal
society thinks it's wrong
what you prefer feels good to you
but exposing it is dangerous
When you're absorbed in their unnatural
it feels good
back to reality now
back to bland
What's right and what's wrong
your inner circle doesn't care
but the outer structure is in control
and you hide
The Internet says it's ok
my friends say it's ok
I feel like it's ok
but the judgment is real
We'll keep hiding in our world of normal
some of us

Impressions
Alison Palmer

To leave our forms behind, the longing that rises, rises
until the dark ceiling of the sky turns us
                    back, and the way we came,
un-riddled with stars.
Miles away, you wake to her, and here,
I wake to her, and we
          ask to be forgiven—it's not the wind's fault
the trees bend in the storm.
                    Aren't we something to marvel at,
lying like fallen branches:
Would my fingerprints disappear from your skin if I
let them find your collarbone, hip
                    bone, curve of your thigh;
          the body's remembrances, fossae, and how lovely
it would be to sign my name where no one else can see.

Her

C. E. Wing

I’ve started on a new journey in life
And along the way, I’ve stopped
For I’m looking for HER
I’ve taken many detours along the way
Only to find heartache, pain and sorrow
But even with all that, I will not stop until I find HER

SHE who is meant for only me
SHE who will complement me
SHE who I so long to adore
SHE who I can shower with my love
I will remain steadfast in my quest
I will remain positive in my search
No amount of heartache, pain and sorrow will deter me
For I know I deserve someone true, loyal and honest
I will stay positive and let my inner light guide me to HER

There Was Us
Skye Myers

once upon a time,
there was us
you with your Irish red curls
your ghosts and your pierced nipples
weed tea, hourglass form
me with my black fingernails,
scarred arms and cigarettes and
forest eyes you would write poetry
about getting lost in
with our love shining like starburst
there were no rules that
we hadn't gone against, were there?
there was nothing that could scare us
into not wanting to tell the world
that we were goddamn crazy
about each other
but as is the way of faerytales,
sometimes things end
before they have a chance
to truly begin

Choose Any Angle You Like, She Said

Alison Palmer

my heart has been here before, knows its way
                    through any field to the woods (there's
always a field, the woods, safety). Leaves take
          turns disappearing in winter, and she
moved so slowly toward me I couldn't tell
what was want and what was merely action.
If the world split in two, she said, what side
                    would you be on? I wanted to answer, yours,
forever, and, of course. One side rages
          fire, she said, the other begs the tides.
I decided to sing a requiem, since my
illusions never stay. She was
                              a contrived storm inside me,
          some great wind that asked me elsewhere, only
to strip me of the map.
Need for protection, I stared down
                    the trees. She broke my song. I am
violent to your heart, she said, the woods, now
          flaming, now drowning, turn you away

Sisters of The Four Winds

Sean Heather K. McGraw

Sisters of the four winds—North, South, East and West
Sisters of the Winding Way
Women of the Western Watch
Watch with us today.

Sisters of the four winds—North, South, East and West
Grandmother, gentle, speak your words
And your Grandmother too.
Sewing the vastness of space into time
Threads colored in every hue.

Sisters of the four winds—North, South, East and West
Carry my burden as I carry yours
We too shall become one.
Sisters who loved one another,
Watching the women run

Sisters of the four winds—North, South, East and West
Vision or dream—or real, maybe,
Faces of Sisters long past and near
I am your descendant-girl
Let me love without any fear.

Sisters of the four winds—North, South, East and West
Sisters of the four winds
Sisters of the Shining Way,
Grant us peace and pleasure,
And good hearts that are gay.

Forehead Kiss
Vanessa Rowan Whitfield

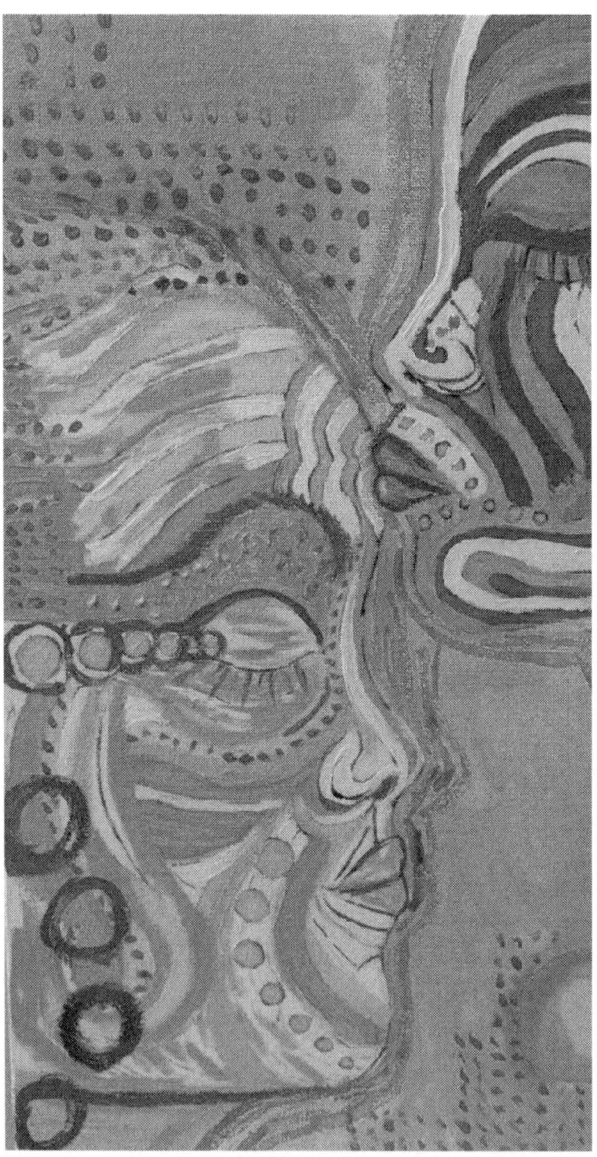

Lady's Fan
Carrie Lee Connel

A cooling breeze
passes over my skin.
A flutter of embossed paper:
turquoise and white lace.
In between bouts of fanning,
you droop,
appear to sleep,
then moan yourself awake
to start the flutter again.
They call your name: Maria.
Tall, almost spindly;
the cruel bully may say "giraffe."
Skin the shade of creamed coffee
yet touched with orange syrup –
perhaps too long under a sunbed
or a mishap with spray tan.
I think you beautiful;
wonder if your age is close to mine.
Are you ill? Is it a hot flash?
Is it anxiety as I feel,
anticipating the next test?
We are a community of women –
waiting to know if the future
holds a journey none of us wish
to embark upon.
My own fan sits at the bottom
of my purse,
anticipating the brimstone burning
of the sermon come Sunday.

First published in *Synaeresis*, Issue 7, Harmonia Press, 2019

Medusa

Destiny Killian

Suddenly, I see her
and I am struck still as stone
She laughs as she runs,
brushing a hand through her tangled hair
I am wild with envy at the fingers
that graze her skin
She knows her own power, and I am
Powerless before her

Men called her a monster, a threat
But all I see before me is Beauty
Can't they see the shimmer of her scales
The glint in her eyes that stops me cold
or the lingering smile on her lips
that breaks my statuary heart before
making it beat again

She is the keeper of the temple
Athena's faithful servant
But it is her who I wish to worship
I would commit every blasphemy,
defend her from every lustful gaze,
and forsake every ungrateful god
To pursue the love of the Gorgon
Medusa, I've come home

When She looks at Me
Paula Jellis

In the golden morning
of her smile
In the quiet silence
between sentences
everything is clear
when she looks at me
In the afternoon
of her kiss
in the dark green shadows
she covers me
and fills me
with desire
In the clear blue light
of evening
the world
falls away
When she looks at me
I think
I can see
eternity
When the deep purple night
wraps me in her arms
I become lost
in the space
between her breath
and mine
In the midnight of her caress
silver, black and endless
my body rises to her
drawn like a magnet
drawn like magic
When she looks at me

Waiting for you to read my mind

Candice Louisa Daquin

There is
an abacus
counting sense and nonsense
on the high cheeks of a woman
who is done saying what she's told.
The photographer
catches her unease
in the shape of her mouth
(it would taste of raspberry, that's obvious).
At night, the crystal of your half-filled glass shines
ice melting slow, like peeling clothes
staring at naked ghosts with their hands up
sexing on dirty carpets with clean minds
watching flashbacks of regrets and pleasure
idling trucks melting snow with their hung-over breath
if you were a pill, I'd O.D. on your potency
skipping heartbeat, chasing down roads, your diminishing form.
You left one day intact and never returned
sending a doppelgänger
a confidence artist, in your stead
who told me; I like your eyes they're untamed
with a paper tongue and windscreen brow
wiping away the rain, that endlessly fell
we must get used to death.
In each pause, in the rhythm of immolation
I touched your skin
and thought of New England apples
the first taste
belief comes last
use your imagination.
Can you see me?
I'm standing waist deep
waiting for you to read my mind
like you did once with the alacrity of a gymnast

in the throes of passion
braille, Morse code
signs and wonders
photos wet and over exposed
ringing telephones in abjuring night
knowing the destination in your fingers and finding
without map or lights switched on, blacking out cries.
To be found, oh God
to be found again
by you.

Elegy for the Unisex Pen
Melissa Fadul

Dearest Bic People,
Thank you so much for the pink and purple rollerball ink pens made just for women! My wife
and me have bought all our friends them!!! Also, thank you for not including directions on how
to remove the cap and trusting that we would figure it out. Why did it take so many years for
your company to produce these feminine pens? Furthermore, how did you manage to get them
to fit in our palm so cozily? Other pens don't sit as well. What could feel more important than
fitting into something?

Sincerely,
A Lesbian

February 10
Laura Elizabeth Casey

This year they made a movie
with your name as the title.
A story about one woman,
weary from convention
in love with a younger one,
full of angst and ecstasy.
An entirely different story from ours
but strange to recognize you and I
like in a daydream.
This year you turned 55,
and like every year
I thought I'd forget your birthday--
that this year would be different.
But instead I dreamt of you, and
I was 22 and you were 31,
time spiraling like pinwheels in a storm.
This year I turned 46
and most days, I've forgotten
being 22.
But when you turned 55,
the memories rushed over me
Like pounding surf and riptide,
pulling me under.
Always pulling me under.
This year I visited the city where
I last saw your face.
Gone is the warehouse dive bar
where we danced to "I Will Always Love You."
My brain a stone tablet of memory—
the brick walls, the cigarette smoke and
the scent of your neck.
This year I slept a few miles from
the frigid basement apartment
where I learned every curve of you.

The pieces of our past and future
become part of me as I sleep. Then morning.
And the pieces fall away.
This year I turned 46,
but you are always 31.
Like a movie character, never to age.
You are always the age you were
when I was 22 and
we danced and froze and slept
in Cleveland in winter.

Isla Mujeres
Sophia Healy

I saw your little face
pass through the courtyard,
sad like the lonely moon
passing through the sea.
I wanted to call out –
climb up here
to the balcony, where the birds sing.
To the tree tops. But your little face
kept walking, crying:
For the injustice they did me, you said,
they'll have to make bricks
without straw.

a sincere and tender passion

Tekla Taylor

our story is
love despite shadows,
hope against hope.
that loneliness still wells up in me now
mostly from the photographs,
her hand around
her waist,
her fingers in
her hair, laughing
or somber
or heavy-lidded with the needy
hope i know.

do not explain
what i know.
I recognize myself with ease–besuited tomboys,
each adoring glance
And candid-shot embrace;
times change, but we don't.
we've been desiring, desirous,
since before they bothered to name us.

at six i was enraptured
by my teacher's golden hair.
no higher pleasure
than to braid it,
small pulse quickened at the thought.
at twenty-six the eyes of my beloved
are golden, amber, moss - she looks at me
as if i am a figment
or a dream.

how could we help but doubt ourselves
when there's so much to disbelieve-

some shadows sheltered us,
even as the shame pollutes the air.

now I shout my love out loud.
i reverberate
to earlier lovers,
fearless in their
nitrate-past and black and white caresses
polaroids of wandering hands, blushes
and crackling letters, delicate folds

where ink might fade but wanting never does.
every bit of evidence, each word, feels like a touch.

The Cycle

Liz DeGregorio

When I want a girlfriend, I do The Cycle.
I cycle through five people in a week,
Five dates, five chances at
        everlasting   happiness
But really, it's misery.
The woman who showed me her collage of infamous murder scenes,
The one who told me a detailed account of a dog disemboweling a rabbit.
The one who described herself as a pimp.
The one who dropped so many racial slurs.
The one who created a love shrine to me in her dimly lit apartment.

The Cycle isn't ever a good idea,
        really.
I've dined out on these stories.
The last Cycle I did, I almost cancelled on
        the last prospect,
        too weird and wired on sugar.
I went anyway.
I had never seen a more beautiful girl.
I asked her, "Do you like to read?" she said no.
She said to me, "Do you like sports?" I said no.

We stared like we were already in love.

Catalyst
Michelle Paige

I haven't been but two thirds full
or maybe five eighths
so brimming (my heart) here is new
and uncomfortable
stretched and used, my love
like an untie-able water balloon
is filling to burst
and I'm not sure (I'm sure)
un-shirt me and stay
because of all the places I've been
in your arms is becoming a favorite
and of all the things that I've seen
the way you look at me
like I'm a new set of crayons on the first day of school
makes me think
that I can finally feel different

Magnetic Hearts
Sarah Vermillion

I’ve been searching for the ways into your heart again,
wondering if I’ll find a way to fuck it up til then.
Though you’re apprehensive to let me under your skin
knowing how it feels to let you go, I’ll let you in.
Eyes of dark caramel, so sweet.
Frame of Aphrodite carved in marble under my sheets.
Your mind, a labyrinth expanding exponentially,
intoxicates and elevates my senses radically.
Our neurons are affected,
‘cause baby, we’re electric.
I’ll keep coming back to you.
I know you feel this, too.
We’ll keep pulling each other even when we’re far apart
I’ve known it from the start.
We’ve got magnetic hearts.

Stridulation Sonnet
Jessica Jacobs

Tiger beetles, crickets, velvet ants, all
know the useful friction of part on part,
how rub of wing to leg, plectrum to file,
marks territories, summons mates. How
a lip rasped over finely tuned ridges can
play sweet as a needle on vinyl. But
sometimes a lone body is not enough.
So a sapsucker drums the chimney flash
for our amped-up morning reveille. Or,
later, home again, the wind's papery
come hither through the locust leaves. The roof
arcing its tin back to meet the rain.
The bed's soft creak as I roll to my side.
What sounds will your body make against mine?

Attempts to Summarize Nine Years in a Page

Eimear Catherine Bourke

First there were bubble-gum candy shoes and a low-slung ponytail
You. Standing in the hallway of a dorm filled with 2011 college girl energy.
Which you were lacking.
Half nervous. Half apathetic.
I had my own reasons for coming out to say hi.
In bed with a beautiful boy. But wanting any excuse to get away.
Unhurriedly yet firmly a friendship formed.
Small gestures like doing one another's dishes. Chatting over popcorn and MTV.
Invariably leading to hangovers, and four friends in a single-bed.
Time trundles on.
Priorities and personalities change.
New sexualities and new focuses are found.
There are drugs, lights and endless amounts of paperwork and studying.
Sometime mid-2013 (I think); we come together on a peeling couch
In a friend's apartment on Cork Street
And after that nothing is quite the same.
Not wanting the sex. Not wanting you.
Wanting to hurt another person. In a far off place.
But
alea iacta est
The death knell of one form of friendship
And the beginning of a new era.
The "Complicated, What's Going on Years?"
I wouldn't take them back.
Memories of phone calls that lasted 'til the early hours of the morning.
I'm a lawyer now. And you're in pilot school in Spain.
Soft water, hard sand
It's 2016 but we're watching a 2003 Louis Theroux documentary over Skype.

SMITTEN

In the laptop screen glow and the breath in my earphones, I could tell you anything.
But I can’t. There is so much not said.
But only sometimes.
Other times there is nothing there. We’re just watching neo-Nazi children play guitars at 4am.
Every time you’re home we’re holding hands beneath bedsheets.
Is this normal?
I feel like I’m losing my mind. And losing all sense of what our friendship once was.
And talking to you is like talking to a wall.
So in 2017 I pick freedom. After that I don’t talk to you at all.
Until 2019. When things aren’t quite so raw.
When we meet for a formal coffee I can still see that nervous teenager in your eyes
What do you see when you see me?

Sunburned Shoulders

Katherine DeGilio

She turns to me with a moan and pulls down her sleeve.
The red and whites of this morning's adventure speckle on her shoulder,
and while she gripes about the pains of having the sun so close,
I cannot help but feel jealous.
I wish I could be near enough to leave a mark,
to be anywhere near her delicate body,
even if only to pull and flake away.
Apollo should be so lucky as to witness how his sun shines down on her skin,
glistening with the perfect serenity of daybreak.
And as she applies aloe to her sunburned shoulders
and hopes that the pain will subside,
I look up at her, for she is my own personal sun,
and I think how lucky I would be to wither in her presence.

Oasis
Milena M. Gil

The tales of old speak
of love that is fire, that is raw
and red-hot and dangerous
Of passion that drives men mad
you are not that
for me
You are my soft, fleece-lined bed
when outside winter hits whip-harsh
against my skin. You are
my resistance to the world
My rest when I am weary
my healer when I am sick
Better than a thousand bleeding hearts
is your warm hand in mine

Memory of You
Jill Lee

Crushed rose petals on my bed,
Sweet memories of you.
The passion has faded,
My love still remains.
You have gone away,
To where I do not know.
Every night it plays out,
My mind cuts and rewinds,
An infinite loop.
Your presence is felt,
My moaning is real.
Where are you my sweet?
I long for your kiss,
My body aches for your love.
You vanished like a ghost,
Leaving me here alone.
All I have are these faded roses,
And the memory of you.

Winter and Spring
Millie Saint-James

	Sometimes it's so hard to talk to you because each time I open my mouth
December 2	swallow myself whole again and again and again my mouth stretches open and I am consumed
	Being with you is like breathing
26 January	I don't even think about it But when I do Everything goes wrong
	I want to give you the world but I can't so I give you my eye
orbs	because it is also a globe no one wants an eye and we are both disappointed
	I forgot my keys
Jaroslava	ya tebe koxayu Because it's spring a miluyu te
	you are the lilacs in bloom the sound of an old man
koxana	playing accordion in the street and the taste of brioche on my tongue you are spring, come at last

peppermint and rosemary

Sarah Karowski

the way her hair wisps
over her shoulder
as she turns,
half smile—
the fastest way
from point A to B
has never quite
been an option
for me.
butterflies eat away
my stomach lining
I find myself caught
in her hair's tangles;
history speaks
of the women who
jellied the knees
of powerful men.
do I envy the women?
or the men?
tangerine and cinnamon:
my mama's pastor
told me god gave me
this heart for a reason
but,
how can I think of anything
when she bites the tip
of her nail? finger teetering
on soft pink lip—did she catch
me staring?
your hair is pretty today
is the straight way
to say
you're a goddess
walking among mortals

I Don't Know How to Flirt, So
Maria Gray

Wednesday morning comes
like an elementary school recess bell,
and you have a black eye. I don't know where you got it, but I have an educated guess.
Nothing that happens here is perfect, but you are eating breakfast again,
and that's the next best thing. Your hair is curly after your shower,
sloppy and secured by a spiral plastic thing
that doesn't hurt your scalp, unlike a band. Try it, you tell me.
It's great. No headaches.
You voted yesterday, and you have the sticker to prove it. It falls off in the wash, same place I lose my favorite socks.
I don't know how to talk to you. I just know I want to.
Who knew you'd love a clump of cells so much? Who knew you could love
something not quite inanimate, characterized by what could be,
extractable with a coat hanger? I cannot love the things
I fit inside of. I love whatever fits inside of me,
begrudgingly. This is your world
and you don't like living in it. Trash litters the lawn.
I hope the ducks don't feast on it. The seagulls are gone
with yesterday's rain. I do not know how this will end,
but I want to be there for it. I hope you feel the same.
Tell me what you love and why,
Ohana, tell me how much or little you miss home
and why your mother deserves better. Tell me about
your best friend's bathroom floor, grime sunken between
the Spanish tiles, and all the times you've laid on it, defeated and post-puke.
You like kissing girls, you say, because they giggle too much
and have to take a break. Her mom is your mom in all manners but blood.
She is straight, your best friend, and you both keep toothbrushes in the other's bathroom.

This Is What Loves Looks Like

In high school, you slept in the same bed, toes intertwined
and alarm set for six-thirty the next morning. You distracted her
when her dog was dying. You entertained her with top-notch DJ skills
when her infected nose piercing demanded a saltwater submergence
and she couldn't look at her phone. You loved her
and scraped yourself off the pavement in ribbons,
because there is no love greater than the love
that knows no prior comparison. With what do you measure the ruler?

Crowned with Love

Angie Waters

Excavation
Kim D. Bailey

this sacred place is what the locals call the landfill what i used to call
a dump once covered with banana peels and coffee grounds
          like kelp and shell on the edge of the ocean. i covered it up
sometimes with a shovel   carried across my shoulder desperate
for the refuse to retreat so i could plant a few flowers before
my roots began to show.   gray and decaying in dying light
lingering in the song of a mockingbird.
she is
          above me this morning, her tail feathers flapping up
and down, flitting from branch   to branch while she keeps an eye
out. i've brought my tithes and candles, a plastic shovel
and bucket hoping they will be
                    all i need.
the harvest moon reaches me here on hands and knees
appearing to pray before i break
the soil
breach the no trespassing sign, and dig.
my back is a table for my sins
               once erected to false gods promising
redemption, upholding stones of sorrow up around the shoulders hunched
over this wounded
earth where
will my flowers grow?
i catch myself holding my breath, why do i do that why do i do   that?
my plastic shovel breaks my heart isn't in it
the soil is too rocky, enraged   i rake at the earth   it's been
too long too much pain
too much time lost to hope   i bleed it out i bleed
i know what's better
it's time to let it
breathe.

Originally Published by *Anti-Heroine Chic*, 2018

The Feathering Sleep

Tara Caribou

nights on nights I lay awake
alone and longing for your arms
your gentle touch
the stroke on my cheek
crystals lay upon my face
make their way to my pillow
I miss you here
behind closed eyes
I see you your hair
spread across your pillow
your soft breathing
the slow spread of your smile
as our eyes meet
I would reach over and caress your shoulder
down your arm and over your hip
you would brush my face
with the back of your hand
I love you, you whispered
before we fell into each other's arms
soft sensitive lips and
whimpers rising
every night I fell into
the feathered sleep of love's embrace
peace and dreams and
your arms and legs
cradling my heart, my body
I remember
running my fingers through your hair
and the way your skin smelled
with my own scent
intermingling with yours
I love you, I always have
and I miss you
more than you could ever know

The Phoenix

Crystal Kinistino

To lovers born to me that now are dead,
I become that other thing,
a burnt offering, the phoenix of new beds

Every dawn I rise,
like an early-bird casualty
minus the worm

Free from the hook which dangles,
torn from the root which strangles

I'm burning like volcanoes,
on this field of scarecrows,
letting only the blackest birds through

this is what happens when they love you,
when they love, love, love
until your hands turn to onyx

When they cremate your kisses,
when they incinerate your caresses,
until your love
turns charcoal,
turns molten,
turns furious,
turns to dust,
turns to fentanyl,
turns to spider veins,
turns to an abscess,
turns gangrene,
turns obscene,
turns promiscuous,
turns to Jesus,
turns to slot machines,

turns to rye & Coke,
turns to a joke,
turns to switchblades,
turns to serenades,
turns to balustrades,
turns Parisian,
turns bohemian,
turns Bourgeois,
turns kamikaze,
turns to classical music,
turns tragic,
turns to death glares,
turns Greek,
turns to a woman,
turns to a man,
turns intellectual,
turns transsexual,
turns to PTSD,
turns to LSD,
turns to pyromaniacs,
turns to panic-attacks,
turns to chain-smoking,
turns to choking,
turns to BDSM,
turns to therapists,
turns to artists,
turns to Carcinoma,
turns to a college diploma,
turns to dyslexia,
turns to anorexia,
turns to insomnia,
turns to candle holders,
turns to cold shoulders,
turns to sinew,
turns to a Jew,
turns to frost,
turns into a holocaust,

the sort of holocaust that
only a phoenix could survive

nothing will extinguish my flame!

To lovers born to me that now are dead,
I've turned into this other thing instead,
the firebird who makes of your pale offerings;

something incandescent,
something iridescent,
something phosphorescent,
something glowing,
something growing in spite of your wrongs,
something with deathless feathers
and tattooed songs.

Shadow
Emily R. Jones

The words within me are for you
Falling forth forming anew
Blank sheets of paper are never there
Your face exists on each page that is bare
The syllables form with you in sight
Spinning words that can take flight
Emotions suppressed waiting for respite
Each sentence bringing a little light
Somewhere to take each word
Make them written and somehow heard
A name unwritten but always there
You take my heart and leave it bare
Never spoken or even said
Your essence is what has always led
The complete of my sum
It is your will always done

A song for a siren

Jesica Nodarse

Moon light haired siren
Queen of my heart
You sang your song
You danced in the waves
I was so scared to swim your way, yet your soul held my hand
I was lost
And you found me
Pulled a string and made my heart double in size
You spoke your truths and nothing will ever be the same
I found belonging and it whispers your name
Your love washes over me
Heavenly waves
My fire I pledge to you
My ice too
Sit by my side
Two queens who'll rule the kingdom of outcasts
Just promise me your waters, will never leave my sands

The Passenger's Seat

Jennifer Mathews

Riding shotgun after
midnight pancakes at Denny's,
she called out piddiddle
and leaned toward me, waiting.
I stretched, seatbelt pulled tight against my ribs,
and I quickly, gently,
kissed her right cheek.
She laughed, kept driving,
turned up Billy Joel. And dropped me off
at home.

I spent nights laying awake
stomach tense, breath short,
picturing myself
in the passenger's seat.
I'd be the first
to spot a car with
one headlight out, shout
piddiddle! I'd lean in
my left cheek leading
then as her seatbelt moved my way
I'd snap my head, lips head-on,
the "accidental" kiss at last.

We spent hours
pumping the player piano
until our legs ached and our heads
were dizzy.
Singing showtunes
as paper lyrics rolled down.
On that piano bench,
I told her
I'd marry her
if I could. But

on my way to college,
I asked
the ultimate question:
If you were stranded
on a desert island
who
would you want to be stranded with?
She said Michael,
I said you
We played a new
driving game
the rest of that summer.
At each stop sign, I'd say
turn right or
now take a left
and we'd drive and drive
through the neighborhoods.
When she had enough
she'd stop the car,
ask How the hell
do we get out of here?
and I'd shrug, hoping
we just might
be lost.

Remnants of One Fire

Kim Harvey

charred mattress
boxes of blackened damp papers
scorched dresser
half-melted floor lamp in the dark

Was someone smoking in bed;
is that something people still do?

My mother does – telltale burn marks
on the sheets

and my father following behind her
stamping out cigarettes, how many times

he's told us his bedroom caught fire
as a boy like the house next door
when I was five

watching Romper Room
while Mrs. Perrin's son was burned
alive how she moved into our den.

He had been smoking in bed,
flames blooming
bursting from their calyx

like the roses you scattered in a path
from the front door to the bedroom
one Tuesday

when we drank cold beers on our roof
as the sun went down over the Mission

and you made me a plate of fruit

This Is What Loves Looks Like

shaped like a daisy:

sliced strawberry pistil, petals
of dates and soft cheese, kiwi
sepals and leaves

all of it here with me
tonight   in the room where I held
your hand while you slept: uninhabited

houses, the dead and displaced,
their possessions, a struck match

smoke and ember, remnants
of a burning bed.

Falling Toward Winter

Rachael Ikins

My lion-haired woman.
Silver-lit-with-red-hair woman.

Your brows remember girlhood,
punctuate your face, their soft pink arches
visible only in pale north light
from our bedroom window
this winter's afternoon.
Like magic your sleepy cat's eyes.
Sharp-chinned, a lick-your-lips,
Smile-woman.
Shag of fire between your legs
glows hot orange. Even on this dusky day.
Through autumn's cold descent.
I fear spreading winter flatness,
every year, December's bottom.
But, you light me.
My fingers can grip your name.
Halfway through November.
month before Equinox,
Coldest cold ahead. The trees,
naked as I. Combed clean of sweat,
memory, they sing a dark song while
I spread my stark, black
branches. Arrange them over evening's
coverlet and wait. For your falling spark.
My dry tinder.

"emotional closure"
Avital Abraham

you call me 5 days later
asking questions and begging for emotional closure
i give you the answers i
think you want to hear
i can't bear the thought of hurting you more than i
already have
we stutter around how conceptually strange it is
to disentangle our heartbeats from one another
you tell me you can't listen to any music anymore
i tell you me neither

Sonnet
Milly Webster

Her reflection is a blur,
Softened edges and blurred lines,
Her lips set apart tell me, go get her,
Go getter. But I stop. My heart pines,

For that ferocious red hair,
Hipster grown out eye-brows,
The spider web eyelids showing where
She has been, the books she likes to browse,

And how late she stays awake.
Dream like state, she blinks lazily,
The pining slows to a dull ache,
She sees my face, only momentarily
But isn't love at first sight just a game?
For I will never even know her name.

so she's gay now?

Milly Webster

"so she's gay now?"

Being a fetish
doesn't mean acceptance
Bisexual IS: valid
Bisexual IS NOT: Being "woke"
it is not an acceptance letter
that determines a lesbian.
fucking stop
judging people

Originally published by *Paragon Press*, 2019

Aphrodite
Sean Heather K. McGraw

Only in the lightness of her eyes, twinkling as they roved across the museum statue

Did you know how she really felt about our art teacher.

The copy of a Roman copy of a Greek original stood out because the object of praise was naked, unusual, a first of the Hellenistic period, Mrs. Jorgenson explained pedantically.

We, being third graders were easily amused at the nakedness of a woman.

The school field trip of all the third graders, Mrs. Jorgenson's class, Mrs. Valencia's class and Mrs. Forrest's class, was to the city museum, and the statues of Greek and Roman origin. I was entranced.
I kept staring at her trying to imagine myself with her, back in Greece, Aphrodite of Cnidus, sculpted by Praxiteles in the 4th century B.C.E.

Someone long ago wrote a poem about her, "Paris, Adonis, and Anchises saw me naked, those are all I know of, but how did Praxiteles make me?"

Mrs. Valencia hovered behind Mrs. Jorgenson as she spoke, her features slightly darkened in the shadows. In a moment of revelation, I saw her stare at Mrs. Jorgenson and then Aphrodite, and back to Mrs. Jorgenson.

My friend, Jenny, looked at me apprehensively, giggling, like all the other boys and girls. Her luscious brown eyes met my liquid blue eyes—we two only -- knew how Praxiteles had made her. He had made her out of love, wasn't that how all women were made? Mrs. Jorgenson, so wise, always a hug and kiss for us, her favorite children, she would always say to each boy and each girl.
Mrs. Valencia, the teacher next-door, would poke her head in the classroom door sometimes to ask if any children needed to be escorted to the school guidance counselor or the principal or the nurse. If a student

was crying, Mrs. Valencia was always on hand to take any third-grader and listen to their plight.

Jenny and I always knew, somehow, without even talking about it, that Mrs. Valencia stared at Mrs. Jorgenson, just as we stared at Aphrodite. Amused, but strangely curious, longing for something. What? We didn't know.

In the fourth grade I realized that I stared at Jenny like that and Jenny stared at me like that. Mrs. Valencia left the school after that year, we didn't know where or why she went. I missed her happy, bouncy voice, "Anybody need a walk?"

One day I caught Mrs. Jorgenson, reading a letter. I couldn't read what it said very well,

Except for the words "dearest Diana" and "how did Praxiteles make me?"

I saw her smile, her emerald eyes moist with tears. I didn't know why. I knew only that now the teacher next door, Mr. Curtis, had one day whispered to another teacher,

"The parents insisted. It was unseemly. What if the children had seen them together?"

With Aphrodite on my mind, one day, I rode the bus to the next stop and got off, and walked to the museum by myself. Praxiteles, who was he? A sculptor of the most famous statue of a naked woman in ancient Greece. What was the longing like, for Aphrodite?

I moved away the next year and I wondered where Aphrodite moved to. Did she long for Praxiteles, Paris, Anchises, Adonis? I would like to think that, having removed her clothing at the bath house, she would have bathed with the other Greek girls of her time. Perhaps she loved Diana instead of Praxiteles?

Standards
Milly Webster

I Think My Wife Tried to Trick
Me Into Gay Sex
BANG!: Why Women Leave Their Husbands for
Other Women
'not straight enough'
Unexpected Scandal
Bisexual women don't want to be your sex 'unicorn'
strange invisibility
'not gay enough'
All bi myself:
Bisexual branded 'vermin'
came out
Then he got fired
Girl crushes, repressed bisexuality and
bi-erasure

Beautiful Phyliss
Paula Jellis

(Starts out as troubadour style love ballad, then goes into an Irish reel)

(We hear a harp)

With eyes of blue and hair of gold
Beautiful Phyliss, Beautiful Phyliss
with delicate ankle and upturned nose
Beautiful Phyliss, Beautiful Phyliss
She was born to please all men
To marry well, to turn their heads
To please their eye, to take to their beds
That's what they said, that's what they said.
So, they never knew what hit them
When Phyliss up and left them
With a note that said:
"All my debts are paid."
And Beautiful Phyliss, Beautiful Phyliss
Ran off with the chambermaid...

(Faster, with Bodhran, flute, fiddle)
Beautiful Phyliss loved the lasses
Thin or thick, faire or small
Wilde or tame, short or tall
Beautiful Phyliss
loved them all as she loved life
vowing she'd be no man's wife
If their eyes be brown or green
Loveliest woman you've ever seen
With sturdy ankles and big strong hands
Shy and meek or bold and grand
Fair or dark, big or small
Wild or tame, short or tall
Beautiful Phyliss (rat-a-tat-tat)

Beautiful Phyliss (rat-a-tat-tat)
Beautiful Phyliss (rat-a-tat-tat)
Loved...
them...
all!

The Unbelievable
Tre L. Loadholt

I love you.
I do.
Older women intrigue me,
I have tried to decline the
feelings that arise when
I see you--deep, brown eyes
coaxing me out of sleep.
I am tongue-tied around you,
want nothing but the rise
of your breasts blessed by
my lips.

I know you know.
I have counted the number
of times you blink in
a minute and passion seems
to hang from the bridge
of your nose.
I am all too eager to
kiss you there.

The unbelievable--
you and I...
opposites in every way:
old vs. young
northern vs. southern
white vs. black
maybe you were right,
maybe we won't be strong enough
to let this love reign.

but, I am stubborn.
I aim to try,

if you'll let me.

Blind Woman walking Along the Strand to Synagogue

For My Wife

Melissa Fadul

I love this—I can see you watching that woman from our kitchen window—says my wife. You have an aerial view of her. I know you wait to make sure she gets to Shul safely. She adds.

Saturdays, I wake early and lean on the pane to see if the blind woman in my neighborhood has decided to go and pray. I'm grateful the days she appears like an elderly goddess molded from starlight, donning a 1940s burgundy *Victory Suit*. Her jacket with black buttons outlines her less than hour-glass figure. An *A-Line skirt* always lags behind a bit due to a constant gentle breeze that seems to be dragged from the past as well. A Purple Maroon Tam hat sits sideways on her head, while her brunette hair is held together in a silk snood. When she walks the cobblestone path through a nearby garden, the heels of her pumps wobble. On her left shoulder, her handbag sways back and forth as if it's a pendulum. In her right hand, her white walking cane and compass— always her sole companion. With each step she sweeps the cane from left-to-right—dependent only on this silent guide. At the curb, I know she knows how many steps she has to get across a street too many people speed down. I know she knows where cobblestone ends and granite begins.

However, does she know how lucky she is not to have to watch her wife leave for work at two a.m. and vanish into a mural of blackness— a hue that seems to have been invented by my anxiety. She doesn't have to worry about stares and sneers when I kiss her goodbye. Does she feel guilty that she can't drive her mother home from the movies— or witness her limp in puddles of dusk and lean on her less arthritic leg walking up steps to her childhood home? Does she know the respite of not being able to see the faces of the parents on television as they recite a eulogy for their gay son—a young man who was tied to a fence with barbed-wire—whose skull was pistol whipped to the point that birds thought he was a scarecrow. When they tried to land on his head to peck at his straw-like hair, they slipped off.

My blind neighbor has never seen paintings— interpretations of this boy's face when he was left hanging like an autumn ornament in a Wyoming meadow. The police officer who cut the boy loose said his face was sopped in blood except for two streaks of tears that were more like silent sirens or flames burning his cheeks.

Every June when I kiss my mother goodbye and she says, *Happy Pride— just be careful at the parade*, I recall Matthew. Last year on the subway, going to Pride, the one day of the year homosexuals outnumber the heterosexuals, a man holding a Bible sneered at me like I was the devil—I pulled my wife closer to me. At the parade, through my camera's lens, I juxtaposed SWAT standing near a float covered in rainbows and dancers and looked at my wife who whispered in my ear, *I'm scared. Why are they here? I Will Survive* boomed from speakers in the distance.

On Pompano Beach after My Father's Funeral

Carolyn Martin

I'm glad he never knew, my mother says
as we walk the storm-sloped shore, precarious
with angry clouds and wind. My father's gone
and we're deflecting grief with talk
deeper than weather in her Florida,
gardens in my Oregon.

She tells me she's relieved I grew into myself
and never let him know. When all my mates
were feminine, she says she understood
and kept her peace.

Your daughter's stubborn, bright, successful
on her own. Why bother with a man?
She fed my father facts without excuse.
It worked for years, she tells me now,
and she's comforted.

I remind her of Sunday afternoons
when we owned the baseball field. He'd pepper
shots to older guys and I'd snag tosses
home, lobbing them so he could strike again.

I tell her how I loved a cowhide's feel,
my Yankees cap, the smell of leather
in summer heat. And how, at twelve, I toughed
it out when hardballs bruised and stung.
My three sons, he loved to joke
about two boys and me.

Thank God, he never knew, she intervenes
and grabs my arm. The shifting sand unsteadies her.
I stop her almost-fall and tell her how I'm hurt.
Would it have been so bad? my voice on edge.

This Is What Loves Looks Like

Her light blue eyes avoid my green. My father,
her best friend, is dead and here we are, slipping
toward that ancient mother/daughter thing
about who owns what's right.

I hold her while she knocks sand from her shoes
and motions toward the car. But I won't let
it slide. *What if he knew?* I press.
Would that have been so hard?

We stop where sidewalk meets the beach,
stubborn in our stance, awkward in our pain.
I'm holding on until her voice unsteadies me.
You'd lose his love, she claims with certainty.

Without remorse, without regret
my mother, his best friend, shatters me
with what I can't conceive. She pulls away
before my voice can find its words
and stinging winds hit my face.

Previously published in *The Wild Ones*

Love 2

SATU

The Burned Out House We Inhabit

Crystal Kinistino

In the vacant house, charred wainscot a flash of memory captured as a photograph, where I come to greet her in the foyer. She keeps that smile, until my hand reaches to caress, her face as wax melts, her smile drips over the windowpane, forming stalagmites, blistered fingers, burned out heart, her hand emerges from the ashes, "holding my cindery, non-existent, radiant flesh. Incandescent."

In absence of identity, personal keepsakes, years of collecting ourselves, kept in boxes, displayed on shelves, soot where our souls once burned with the vigor of starlight. Caught between rocks, we push together, one breath, hot enough to burn the braid of us, the knot tied from infancy to senility. Somewhere, on the chart of our development, we failed our goals; trust was replaced with mistrust, autonomy with doubt, identity with confusion, intimacy with isolation, and productivity with stagnation.

We were left with these bodies, whose faces are as familiar as strangers, jagged teeth, fading ivory, loss of skin's elasticity, hollowed eyes, lacking glimmer & glitter. We decorate our souls when we can no longer attend the celebration of who we are,
but as we fade far, know that the soul never forgets its purpose. We came born with a song and a reason to sing it, who among us can content herself with a furled feather, clutching a long sleep if we never care to dream or awaken?

My wishes blown out, one final sparkler lights up the dark like a fiery organ, I multiply each breath, resuscitating this smothered heart. Little girls again, we run together, past rolling brooks, leading to the water's edge, here we walk back, retracing ashen steps. I pour lava into the places where we failed to grow, forming from ebony pitch, a shiny onyx tear. We walk the path of tears, and reach the ocean of our separation, in hope of growth, tossing these in the salt water and brine of rejected kisses, cold arms, stern faces,
meter sticks, belts, brutality, and broken hearts.

SMITTEN

We come back none the better, none the wiser,
the same fleck of green, same dark sense of loss,
covering the forest in moss.

But I love her, as I love the earliest memories I have,
the ones where hope thrived in small corners and tables were set
by our imagination, with no real food, no real sustenance,
nothing to nourish us, no hydration, but the one seed planted,
was enough to assuage our thirst, to restore the air again,
to allow for flight, and we rose without thought or fear of falling.

I now know love
Karissa R. Whitson

I never saw
A man
The way I saw her
I never understood
What beauty was
Until I saw her
I never knew
That I was capable
Of this kind of love
Until I met her

Your Hair Hangs Down

Charity M. Muse

Your hair hangs down like wisteria blossoms
The color and fragrance
Overtaking me
I lose myself in the scents of romance and spring
You move over me like the rain
Coming over a soft field of heather
The sweet smell of water and wet
Touching the places of drought and desire
You touch me like a soft breeze
And play with me like the sunlight
Peeking through the broad green leaves
In dappled golden rays
You love me like the sunset
Full of hues, colors, and shades
Full of mystery and magic
So that I never want it to end
We make love like the spring and summer
Dancing leaves, stems, and blossoms
Love and rain and sunlight
Wind and fragrance and stars

The Ballad of the Unrequited Lesbian

A. Lawler

So I have spent the past 45 hours as a wreck.
You wanna know why?
Well, there's this girl and we're almost friends
And we're almost something more.
But that's another conversation.
I'll save that one for another night.
We went out for drinks and we talked.
This is the second time we've done this.
You would think I would have learned the first time around.
But no, she's pretty.
And I... can't think straight.
So, I drink some vodkas with little basil leaves in the glass.
We talk. We share. And in retrospect I hate myself for everything I said.
Why do I pour my guts out every time we drink together? What is wrong with me?
And I wanna be a poet right now.
I want to take that night and all that conversation and make something beautiful out of it.
But I'm afraid that can't be done.
There is no poetry in life except what armchair lovers make up while they're day-drinking.
There's just stupid feelings and embarrassing drunks.
And if anyone tries to tell you otherwise
I have a lifetime of experience to prove them wrong.

Summer 2018
Teresa T. Chappell

The three of us sat
on the patio, our voices
soft so as not to wake
your parents. I could almost
pretend we were
still in high school.
I wondered if either of
you could feel
the new barrier I had
put up. Could you see
the pink & blue ribbons inside
me twist into each other? Did you
notice the collision of pigment
bloom into a lavender field?

Her entirety

Karissa R. Whitson

It is not her hand that is soft
She works away her days
Tired
It is her heart
And her eyes
And the voice she uses
Only when speaking to me
That is the softness of her that I need
It is not her touch
It is her
Entirety

Innocence

Izabell Jöraas Skoogh

She was innocent.
In a way, I haven't found anyone to be.
The way her fingers closely touched my skin,
like she was inspecting every inch of me and didn't want to miss out on any of it.
She touched my naked skin, carefully, like I was something she was afraid to break.
I had never experienced it like this, but it was all I had ever wished for.
I never wanted anyone to throw themselves at me not caring about how fragile I might be.
Our first kiss,
so messy,
so not in sync,
so perfect - perfect in the way of how raw and real we allowed ourselves to be.
Nothing that had been practiced for hours on end by meaningless interactions.
She made me so nervous,
and I carefully touched her.
It made me want to taste her lips again,
but most of all,
hear her voice speak her mind.
Damn so beautiful.
I liked how she carefully wanted to touch those parts of me that hadn't been touched before.

The Value of a Rusty Coin

Nick Kay

Two seats ahead,
Redhead,
Not copper but dyed,
Dirty blonde at the roots,
Rusted coin at the ends.
She doesn't shine; newly minted.
Instead she glints,
Like a wish tossed to the bottom of a pool.
Hoard her,
Those little things,
Shades of pink and red and so warm:
Her freckles when she says hello
Lipstick on her teeth
The back of her neck on a cold day
Her loose pants stark
Against her girlfriend's blue jeans
As they kiss, the sweetest color.
Coins change hands,
I don't know the wallets she has belonged to;
The supermarkets she has travelled;
Or the year stamped on her back;
I don't want her,
But I love her nonetheless
For being who
She is:
Hope in the form of the sun,
As I orbit distantly and watch,
What pride and love is like.

Mondays after basketball
Carolyn Martin

we strolled around the high school's factory brick,
passed the soda shop where duck tails smacked lips
with teased-out hair and menthol cigarettes.

Queens of the Court, we owned four counter seats
at Woolworth's 5 &10 and cherry cokes
cooled us off from practice once a week.
That was it: one hour, once a week
with Mrs. Haas drilling us on half-court sets,
quick head-fakes, two dribbles right,
the smooth lay-ups we'd bank our victories on.

And every time those senior boys jeered
our under-handed foul shots, she taught
us how to earn respect. *Stay in the game,* she'd say.
Ignore those jerks and play.

We listened to her Monday afternoons,
then took our game to dances Friday nights
where priests and nuns roamed the gym
to cool teen body heat. Every week they'd claim,
The Holy Ghost needs breathing space,
and we would cheer that claustrophobic Ghost
and throw *Great balls of fire!* at boys whose sneers
rolled off our backs. We had game and held our own.

I loved these girls who never smelled of smoke
or Jean Naté or shared their spit with guys.
Before the buses sent us home at night,
we'd laugh our glasses dry and couldn't wait
to hug hello before the morning's school bell rang.
The last to leave our stop, I'd spend my time alone
replaying swished jump shots, reveling
in confidence I banked our friendships on.

But then one night, competing in my head,
I almost missed her passing by: a red suit
in black high heels, chestnut hair, oval face,
the easy gait that whispered, *Feminine*.
I couldn't free my eyes or catch my breath,
or calm the roused-up parts I never knew.
Fumbling for my blue gym bag, I hopped
a bus – heading who knows where – and slumped
into a back-row seat. The streetlights held
no clue what this was all about, what this
was yet to mean. And neither did my face,
shocked and curious, reflecting back at me.

Previously published in *Paper Nautilus*

on giving away too much

Cassandra Bumford

this girl, with brassy eyes,
asks me for a favor.
she is heavy with sedative,
pleading with me, please,
just take the pills.
she doesn't want to see them,
tells me she's going home soon.
she does not ask if i can take
the pills and not
take
them.
i never learned the colors
of the walls inside her head,
but i remember the etchings
on her forearm and smelling
of her shampoo. a few pills
still sit in a tea tin hanging
in my room. i am so proud
that she is not a ghost,
but hate that she haunts me.

Merveilleux

Charity M. Muse

You are the subject of every love song
The inspiration behind every note
Driving the melody into my heart.
You are the study of every painting
The technique behind the strokes
Coloring my life's expression.
You are the beauty of every story
The climax and resolution
The perfect novel enchanting me.
You are the heart of every poem
The rhythm and the rhyme
Adding beauty and mystery to my life.
You are wonderfully beautiful, merveilleux
The love of my life
The one I am after.
Hear me.
Hear the words I dare not speak
Yet call out to you
Every time I look into your eyes
Hear me say "I love you"
In the little kindnesses and sweet words
In the lingering around just so I can,
However briefly, be alone with you.

My Way Home
Marie Prichard

Sixteen years of tears dripping into the void of an unfortunate choice
that circled my ring finger.
A spirit without a home
broken and in pieces.
Shards of bitterness cutting unwelcome skin
pressed against mine.
Wanting, needing, aching to reclaim lost time
ricocheting across an expanse.
Shadowy glimpses of truth
brushed away for a moment.
Only to return as a steady thrum
in the space between my thoughts, my breath, my soul.
Lost on long, empty trails of confusion
cliffs lined with jagged rocks.
Following straight lines with hard, masculine edges
leading me further away.
Rumbling aftershocks
shifting the landscape.
Straight lines softening, meandering slowly, entwining
Allowing for the touch of her gentle hand.
A softly spoken voice
keeping time with the beat of my heart.
Erasing my tears, my bitterness, my confusion.
She whispered my name and I found my way home.

I am the age of innocence
V. Hamilton

I am as different as a daisy growing thru the gray sidewalk crack
The world may be full of daisies but none to which I can see
The world is as small as I am
I know I am alone
A tiny seed of you is inside me

I am the age of wonder

The difference grows wider
The awareness grows heavy
Will it ever change
Can dreams that are the same, yet too different to speak of be valid?
Where are you?

I am the age of rebellion

Becoming who I know I am
Hidden from the world or so I think
Screw you
Yet I conform
Who am I?
Do you exist?

I am the age of my surroundings

I long for you but you're elusive
I settle in to get the job done
I go through the motions
Life flows like a fish swimming upstream
I look forward to what comes after the spawn
I guess I can’t find you

I am the age of fulfillment

SMITTEN

I know what should be left behind
I see beauty where I once saw concrete
Other flowers bloom thru the cracks
The ocean mist feeds me

There you are
I found myself

I found you

I am the age yet to come

Is it all a dream
Has the seed sprouted into a beautiful black haired goddess
You seem as real as the sun that warms my face
Inside the fire burns my soul
Unable to breathe
Unwilling to be anything but your loving servant
I can’t lose you

I am the age of my grand finale

What a life we've shared
Our garden blossomed
Our faces cracked with lines of laughter
The gray has subsided for the flowers
I held you close and you loved me

You were always there

True Colors
Erin King

I dip the brush dreamily into red.
One line, from thigh to knee.
My canvas stretched before me,
You are pink and white -
Curved calves and breasts.
Violet swirls down to graze your toes
Ultramarine in your clavicle's hollow,
Sweet umber around each wrist.
You suck in your bottom lip
Curl your fingers helplessly
Wondering where I will paint next.

The Stranger
Jennifer Carr

The unnamed woman who stands
in sunlight dancing upon the grass
the view from across the park
her angles and curves
teasing my tunnel vision
my steady heartbeat gone
my heart suddenly in dysrhythmia
as I let my mind wander
is her tongue peppery
from the BBQ ribs
grilled on this Memorial Day
one I won't forget anytime soon
as I quietly let myself gaze
behind my dark shades
wondering what her name is
fantasizing about our first date
trying not to think about
what it would be like
for me and you
to become us

Words
Charity M. Muse

She said she needed me to tell her exactly how I feel toward her. My heart pounded in my chest,
and blood rushed to my palms as sweat formed in little droplets on my head, revealing my angst.
I managed to whisper, "I'm afraid."
She moved in closer, took my hand and leaned her head toward mine, leaving just enough space
between our lips so I could feel her breath on mine.
Like one magnet to another, I was drawn in, and soon I felt the damp softness of her wide smile
against my lips. I touched the side of her face with my left hand, while I caressed the locks of her
hair with my right.
We connected. At last. There would be no turning back.
I kissed her tenderly then smiled just before we laughed together. Then, in a low quiet voice, she
said, "now use words."

Je ne regenette non
Hallelujah R. Huston

Je ne regenette non

no regrets
I flew for a moment
in the space between
her lips

Evanese

this will disappear
from memory
the way her hand
fit in mine
a bird in nest

the death of sparrows
fallen hard
our loose feathers
mingled in mid-air
for a moment
before we
smacked the ground

Then

miraculously
my heart
beat
again

The Ologies
Sarah Bigham

I.
I am a teacher and a writer and an artist and a gardener and a cook and a reader and a piano player and a compassionate friend. I dream and sing and wrap myself in words, comforted by the many ways to express situations, thoughts, remembrances, and feelings. My sentences are long and my thoughts ping from one subject to another while I do crossword puzzles and talk to family members on the phone. My world runs on emotion and how I feel at any given moment, life-altering decisions being made in an instant.

My wife is a scientist.
She does not dream (she says).
She likes clear communication.
She prefers concise language.
She thinks rationally.
She uses data.

She lives in a world of science and her work involves terms I do not understand and instruments I do not know how to operate, let alone turn on. (She insists on the use of "instruments" when I try to say "machines." The word instruments makes me think she spends her time surrounded by piccolos and snare drums.) From the first time we met, I found her ways interesting and loveable, quirky really. I loved her calling in science because I loved her. Science was not a part of my world, not a component of my thought process.

And then I got sick.

II.
She spoke the language of experts
in cardiology, dermatology
hematology, gastroenterology,
gynecology, neurology,
ophthalmology, pharmacology

and urology.
She became my interpreter, my guide, in this land of the Big Science, as I often think of it, a place where I frequently feel overwhelmed and unworthy, bumbling and rushed, easily confused by the clipped, unfamiliar language devoid of the nuance and lyrical cadence normally swirling around me.

She navigated routes to appointments.
She made solutions for treatment instillations.
She calculated half-lives of meds.
She read research papers.
She collected data.
She charted my pain.

I saved my words for my sisters and my writing colleagues and my close friends and the people next to me in line at the pharmacy, as well as the acupuncturist and the counselor and the cranio-sacral massage expert and the yoga instructor and the meditation leader, whose services I needed just as much during this medical odyssey. But they were more of my world, and not the Big Science. I cried and we talked and they assuaged my pain in different ways.

I have learned the importance of both worlds.
I need and love the Big Science.
I need and love my wife.
They both have saved me.
She holds my hand.
And I am healing.

Originally published in *Touch: The Journal of Healing*

The Cure for Everything

Carol H. Jewell

"I know the cure for everything: Salt water…in one form or another: Sweat, tears, or the sea."
—The Deluge at Norderney, Seven Gothic Tales, 1934 (Karen Blixen/Isak Dinesen)

I.
Back
b
 r
  e
   a
    k
     i
      n
       g
pulling or pushing
to get
something out
bandana on your head
or
sunhat, dripping
your face
your eyes
the summer garden
the labor bed.
II.
How long do I cry for
all
of
you
how many shirtfronts
are drenched
red eyes RED EYES
hair mussed

snot smeared
a sting, a long ache:
the unending bellow.
III.
I know you dislike
sand between your toes
most fish, shellfish

I put on my w i d e
brimmed hat
take your hand
walk in the low tide
until it's time to go;
the sunset.

Rose Quartz

S. A. Quinox

She's delicate like the petals
of a cherry tree
at its full blossoming pinnacle.
She's all soft shades of pink
that linger upon the tip
of my pleading tongue.
Thus I keep her
in my wildest of pockets
close to the membranes of my heart;
like the rose quartz
beneath the silk of my pillow,
like my arms around her thighs.

Ode to what could have been my first kiss
Kirsten Fedorowicz

I am fifteen when Julia asks if she can be my first kiss.
We are lying on her bed,
the feathered comforter soft on the exposed small of my back,
her heavy pillows bending my neck at an uncomfortable angle.
I look at her, my best friend,
legs long and tightly shaved,
blonde hair permed into curls
by her Grandmother, a hairdresser,
eyes freshly blue with the removal of mascara,
carefully removed two hours before
as I watched, amazed at how she cleans her face with a single swipe,
how everything feels easy to her.
Even the way she curls her eyelashes in the morning,
without pulling out a single hair,
laughing at the way my shoulders shudder
at the curve of the metal, *a medieval torture device* I tell her.
She is looking at me when she insists that
kissing is a sign of affection,
can be a friend thing.
She's started a kiss list,
keeping track of every person she's locked lips with.
By the time we are seventeen,
that list will have more girls than boys,
Girls she's caught on the track, smashing their lips together between laps.
During spin the bottle, reaching for their faces across the circle,
at sleepovers between secrets, after talking about the boys they like,
she'll peck them softly, laugh and say *practice.*
I hold my breath for a moment, staring at the stucco ceiling,
pondering this proposal before saying *no*.
I'm holding out for how I imagine this is supposed to go--boy.
Paul, a family friend, will fall for me someday, it's destiny,
we'll go behind a tree on a family camping trip, and he'll kiss me.
Jesse, who I'll have a crush on for the next three years,

Pining after his perfect calves and soft, wavy hair-
he could kiss me at a Prom or after a band concert,
his drumsticks still tucked in the white of his socks.
At my response, she nods, says *okay, I understand*
says *let me know if you change your mind*,
we both stare at the ceiling together,
the bare skin of our legs touching,
our breath synchronized, soft in the night,
rise and fall of flat, young stomachs,
she turns out the light,
rolls her back to me,
pulling the soft purple blanket with her,
And I don't realize I miss the sound of her
until she has already turned away.

Athena
Mandy Grathwohl

To have the world, all of it,
inside your brain: a recipe for happiness?
Endless sun, you drink the ocean and float.
Not Athena.
She came forth like this:
a terrible union.
Zeus swallowed Metis and nipped the snake in the bud;
his baby boy by her
would topple him, as he had Cronus.
When she swooned he swallowed her;
problem solved.
But there was a terrible knocking:
a headache to end the world.
Zeus screamed and the springs rumbled.
Pompeii puffed.
Zeus screamed
and it was as if
sound would never be again.
Hermes came; he 'tsk'ed his tongue
and had a wedge brought.
Splat! They cracked the skull.
Wider, split the bone, hear the squinch
of pink and slither
and out came Athena:
a full girl, armored up. She did not weep.
Her daddy loved her:
his powerhouse girl, the prodigal daughter.
She only of his blood,
and so she was more perfect.
He let her use his thunderbolts.
He let her be alone.
Here's where the sorrow comes:
virgin Athena, unwanting of boy sex,
who fled Hephaestus when he tried to take her

and swept his cum off in disgust—
was there a want there in the wings, unspoken?
As in, did Athena dream of Aphrodite's body
the way others dreamt of Adonis'?

Hard hands, thunderstruck,
on pale girl flesh. Athena in her cloudy bedroom
and weeping.
Who loves girls except for men?
Wise Athena, lonely owl,
I hope someone secret loved you back.
I pray there was a stable girl
who took the bridle you made
and said thank you with all eyes.
I hope she pet you
like she brushed the horses
and ran her tongue along your secret
unarmored body.
I can keep a secret.
They say you stayed a virgin
but if you loved someone you can say it.
Tell the corners. The owls. The horses.
Tell us what you couldn't then
and take your clothes off.
I'll guide you to the river.
I'll watch out while you wash yourself.
Take a golden girl to the shore
and make her say your name,
show her the sunset over Athens.
Brush her hair back with your teeth.
Learn everything that you couldn't:
the sigh of your name in a high voice,
the river between two thighs,
the way breasts look like mountains
in the right light.

Voca Di Stregil

Vanessa Rowan Whitfield

"I envied you-"

The way she could play
I had wished I were her
on more than one day.

"I envied you-"

Micro-fringe banged angel
banging on a piano
with a built-in music box
pouring out

Like Lucifer,
If Lucifer was
a beautiful woman

"I envied you-"

Raven wings create her
mane
and two red birds make up
a mouth

Their song casts a spell
over all who listen

Stunned
Paralyzed

An audience seized
In angler fish light

Dazed Drugged
Breathing slowed

Frozen in her Medusa gaze
Captured by her honey

Venus Flytrap
Pitcher Plant

I am left senseless
in her trail of syrup

the internal opus
exorcised and bellowing out

Enchantress,
with a symphony that booms
from the chest and lures me
over to the rocks

"I envied you-"

the voice of the clitoris
if only it could speak

she was an anthropomorphic
orchestra
with eyes like towers

I hear her voice,
and it sings through me
I hear her voice
and it sings through me
"I wanted you."

I don't want your pretty

Erin Van Vuren

I don't want your pretty.
I don't want the smile you
paint on for the world.
I want your sadness.
I want your fever.
Give me your fucking storms.
I don't need your black
dress on my floor. Give me
your naked mind. The pieces
of your soul that you're
too scared to show in the
light. I am not the sun.
I am the universe, and
I will swallow your
darkness whole.

- Erin Van Vuren

Family Reunion
Kirsten Fedorowicz

you & I, we both know
what I am. Green grass,
freshly mowed. Picnic tables,
swing sets, sunshine. And,
still, your grandmother introduces me to
every new family member as
your "friend,"
standing there, silently,
as their southern accents fill
the July air, expansive as the homeland
that your mother fled. I understand
why; you never answer their
questions. They never ask anything
important, don't look at me
next to you. You,
wearing a T-shirt and
visible queerness. Me,
a sundress and shyness. You hold
my hand behind your back, folding
our fingers into a fist. You are
nineteen years too angry to
hide anymore, three inches too short
to mask how my body stands by
yours, how I linger like a kiss. Later,
I take the family picture, tucked
behind the lens of a camera
I don't know how to use. I snap
pictures of strangers, capturing their
static laughter. When the family
sends out these pictures
for Christmas, no one will
think of the photographer except for
you, who will remember me
as I am. Green grass,

Freshly mowed, picnic tables,
swing sets, sunshine, silence.

The first title was your name

Isabel J. Wallace

I try to find you when I’m sleeping,
chasing memories with a photo-finish
and the texture of words between the hardback cover
of a book I stole from the library when I was ten.
I remember how you tucked your chin to your chest,
when it was colder than your optimism had accounted for.
I remember the gloss of light in your hair
while we ate breakfast standing up by the kitchen window.
I remember the terror and the promise when I realized
that I’d fallen for you in the span of three bars of sheet music,
when you laughed too hard to hit the right keys,
and I looked so lost at sea that you asked if I needed a lifeline.
But I’ve gone under now;
the current dragged me down and dragged you up.
We reached out and our hands didn’t catch.
There’s just dark pressure and oxygen we can’t use.
It’s the same feeling I get with a nightmare,
and it’s no wonder that I’ve been dreaming of you.
The current dragged me down and dragged you up,
and you always said I was never good at judging directions—
but when I remember the last time I saw your face,
I think I might have learned something about loss.

FemBot– the dynamic of the unspoken role in the unwritten

Sarah Ito

I like the dance,
I think,
Or maybe it is the energy...
I like the door that is opened for me,
The woman who is strong
When I choose not to be.
Maybe it is her look,
Her darkness, sultry,
Sulky, that countenance
That brightens against my blonde being,
The blackness of her eyes shining into my
Blue,
I like the dance,
I think,
Or maybe it is the music...
I hear it, at times,
When she is in my presence...
And ebbs to a quiet tide
Of silence, when she goes away.
I like the dance,
I think,
Or maybe it is the surrender...
The easy parting of my will
To her wants...
I like the dance.

Gatwick [1]
Carla Toney

I stand alone, hands frozen,
nose streaming from the cold,
as I watch your plane turn into
the wind and taxi onto the runway.
May the golden light of love and
the silver light of wisdom encircle you,
protect you, take you safely home,
I pray as your plane hurtles down
the runway, lifts its nose into the air
and disappears southeast
in the morning sun.

I stand alone, hands frozen,
nose streaming from the cold.
Is our love a Catherine wheel?
Sparks fly as the wheel spins,
slows and fizzles to a stop.
Or is our love the moon that
slice by slice disappears
but is never gone?

---

[1] Gatwick is an airport to the south of London, England

s u n s h i n e
Cassandra Bumford

hearing you call her your sunshine hurt
in a way i couldn't expect. not the way
a toothache tastes or the way it smells
when someone else blows out the candles
on your birthday cake;
it hurt how it stings to look underwater,
but oh, i find myself doing it anyway
because the provocative view is worth
the pain. you are salt water in my tear ducts,
but i'm stupid enough to keep opening my eyes.

Home
Sarah Kacala

It's as vital to us, as breathing; this need to find the meaning. This searching for the feeling of being home. To feel such a peace crawl beneath your skin, as it sinks right down and settles in. And nothing is as important as this; as the feeling, of finding home. It's so much more than just four walls and a ceiling. It's something deep within your soul, that gives your whole life meaning. It spreads across your body like wildfire; this sense that hope is never leaving. And you cannot replace it with anything else. There is nothing quite like this feeling.

I spent my whole life searching, and building walls that would always fall. And there's nothing I could do to stop it, and by now I've lost count of them all. I searched for it in sunsets. I searched for it in places so far away. But none of those places felt right to me. None of them beckoned me to stay. I resigned myself to this alienation; to this feeling that I didn't belong. I took comfort in the emptiness I felt deep inside. I held onto it close, for so long.

When she entered my world, she turned it upside down. She peered through my walls with those piercing blue eyes, and they came crumbling to the ground. I stood there amidst those piles of rubble, and all I could see was her. The world around me just disappeared, and everything began to blur. The sound of her laughter, now filled my world. Her smile became my light. The words that she spoke, were like oxygen to me. Her love brought my soul back to life. She took my hand in hers, and held it so close to her cheek. And everything changed inside my heart, as my knees grew feeble and weak.

What was this feeling? Who was this girl? And how had she managed to break down my walls; the ones between me and the world? I loved her the moment I saw her. There was no going back to the way it was before then. She changed my life forever. She's my soulmate, and my best friend. We look out for each other. We care for each other. We laugh hard together, even on the hardest of days. And nothing could change the way that I feel about her. This love, will always remain. I had spent my life searching in all the wrong places. In four walls and ceilings; in decorated spaces. But these precious moments in your life; the ones when the truth comes stumbling out into the light. You cannot possibly imagine what it's going to feel like. And even if you could, you cannot rehearse them. For I had finally discovered the truth for myself; that home was never a place; it was a person.

Maggie

Henri Bensussen

She's shorter than me
and wider, woman-at-large
At the dance, dressed
in black, even the tie, formal
Seductive fashion on display
pulling me in when she looks my way
It happens too often, her glances
drawing my eyes in her direction
When I was younger, years ago
I'd kiss those lips, or sit in her lap
We'd dance a slow dance and later
more could happen, but now
we're both weightier, caught
by pounds of flesh, my frail age
Carrying the weight of wizened
action forsworn—I'd be crushed
by everything she has to offer, yes
her body, her gaze, her expectations

Lilies for Sweetness
Clementine

Roses to pretend I still have mon cœur
Yet the roses as they wilt scream “no it’s hers”
They turn black blue and purple
Like the bruise on my hand, pressed to my mouth

Though lilac gets me wildin
Her perfumed self draws me in
Cheeks pink as a lily fleur
Eyes wider than they were before

Lilies for sweetness
Lily’s own sweetness
It’s like sugar, or stevia
Or whatever my mom thinks is healthy these days

Baby’s breath could never compare
To that maple sugar Lily air
Though like buttercups
She makes my face light up

Dandelion heart of gold
Peony soft hands to hold
But I’ll never do that
Cause my hands are sweaty as the morning dew
Mon amour
You’re the flower I adore
Prettier than a Lily’s core
I don’t understand how you do this to me

Lilies for sweetness
Lily’s own sweetness
It’s like sugar, or stevia
Or whatever my mom thinks is healthy these days

SMITTEN

Baby’s breath could never compare
To that maple sugar Lily air
Though like buttercups
She makes my face light up

Mon fleur,
Je ne comprende pas

Lavender Tea

Skye Myers

bring her tea in the morning. lavender tea, with one spoon of sugar and a dash of milk. she'll make it seem casual but her dancing eyes always betray her joy. don't comment on her wild hair unless it's to tell her she looks like a mermaid; don't hold her hands with their delicate bones unless you plan to gift her palms and dust her knuckles with kisses.

remember that she won't believe you when you tell her she's otherworldly, the most eloquent of all goddesses. tell her anyway. tell her I sent you. and please. if you could, please tell her I loved her best when she wore a crown of paper flowers and fallen stars. tell her I have my heart tattooed to my sleeve now so I can't hide my vulnerability.

tell her she was the most beautiful when she was surprised into laughter and didn't have time to cover her mouth because she was self-conscious of her crooked teeth. tell her I miss her more than I miss the ocean. tell her I still dream of her eyes and her mouth and her horns.

please tell her. tell her again and again that she is the most perfect creature in your world. she doesn't hear it enough and deserves to.

No Distance / No Boundaries
Jack Neece

It was a long drive. I can see she is tired. I smile knowing she made time to see me even though it was out of her way to do so. She lays her head on my lap. We are watching tv.

My head is in the clouds as I run my fingers through her hair. My heart swells as she rolls over and turns into me. She curls herself around me and our eyes meet.

My heart stops as I feel our souls touch. The lines between our bodies blur and my heart finds its rhythm in her chest. I can feel her blood coursing through my veins and mine through hers.

I see, "I love you" in her eyes and nothing has ever been more beautiful. We are one and we travel back and forth in time together. Her breath is the wind my dreams fly upon and I have no more fear.

I have been reborn in this woman. The fire of my past forged a soldier, she has taught me to lay down my weapons.

As I trace her now sleeping face I say a silent prayer: "Let me put all of the love I have into this woman that she may feel even half of what she makes me feel."

I kiss her lips and all is right.

Every lie told
Every sting of an angry hand against my flesh
Every bone broken in hatred
Every heart string cut by serrated blade

Gone
My memory has been wiped clean

She is all that matters

My healing angel
My righter of every wrong
My home

She is my home
I pray every night that I am hers

Ephemeris
Cristina DeSouza

Ephemeral is your body
I imagine at half-light, as the
moon wanes in the horizon.

Ephemeral is my hope in life,
that it will bring me peace and
wisdom to accept and let it all go:

-the scent of your hair mixed
with fresh cinnamon in the mornings.

Ephemeral are my thoughts of love
at midnight, when light is dim
and I can't fall asleep.

Sleepless, my hours
pass, my faith buried in the recess
of my small breasts:

-space I keep for your gentle fingers,
lingering in deep caress.

And if all is ephemeral, I look at the
stars speckled with sky, searching for your
ephemeris, the ephemeris of your signs

I lost somewhere in time, as the mild
Fall night evolves and I dream awake
of your brownish eyes lying on my olive skin…

Secret Admirer

Ruth Bowley

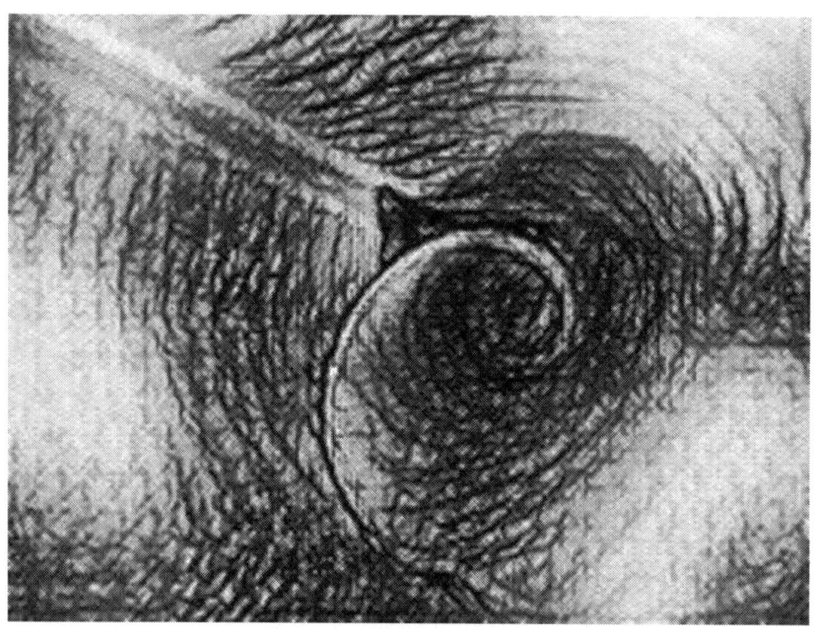

I met her more than once
in my mind.
A lover of which my eyes had designed.
I have infinity been a fairy tale addict until a fistful of mistakes.
This lover though, she held me dear.
Brown eyes with a tint of hell.
A sway to her hips that could cast a spell.
I could give her...my lover no name.
Words to her beauty...would only do shame.
I wore my poverty torn hands on the miracle line between...
negotiable thigh
and
subtle...textures of her rounded backside.
Only then did WE release OUR pride.

Out of the Windfields
Jessica Jacobs

When combines brought the fields
to their knees, it felt like running
an arid spreadsheet. Grid by grid,
I logged my miles, the hours
on my feet, but kept true account of nothing
so much as my loneliness. How long
since I'd been held there,
even by water, given my weight to another?
All winter, the sky was desolate
white of a mussel's middle leached by cold
of its gasoline glimmer. Static
landscape, untongued by tides. Yet constant
as lighthouses were the turbines. Idle,
they were sky-flung starfish
far from the sea, but moving they were
majestic, amphibious animals in their proper
element. Able to arc into the unseeable and return
with power. I tried to do the same.
But instead was desiccated, field-stripped, brittled
down to parts. Then there you were. Beside me
as my headlights slid the storm-slick streets. Submerged
together, a turbine's red light pulsing its beacon
through the rain. Beneath it, your hands
bound me back together. In answering
prayer, I folded myself into the footwell; knelt
between your knees. And
my mouth to you was every water
I'd ever tasted: clean shock
of snowmelt in an alpine pond; tongue cased
in ocean's wetsuit of salt; green and mineral
of a springfed lake—but most of all,
chlorine's high bite in the throatback
of every Florida pool in summer, the water
so bath-warm, so body-kindred, that entering

was like sliding into another skin—skin
that entered you back.

"Out of the Windfields" from *Take Me with You, Wherever You're Going* © 2019 by Jessica Jacobs.

Moonlight

Avital Abraham

you tell me you love the way my love is sunshine
that loving me is sunshine
that I am sunshine
If my love is sunshine,
then yours is moonlight
Your love is a warm bluish silver
reflecting on still open waters
moonlight
your love is finally coming home after a long time of being away
like finally sinking into your own bed
with your own pillow and your own room
comforting and familiar
your heart settling for the first time in what feels like forever
your love is reading a good book on a rainy day
curled up with a soft blanket and a mug of something warm
raindrops pattering gently on the windowsill
already knowing the ending and just delighting in the details
your love is learning something new
something that shifts your rose colored glasses,
your
camera obscura
something that reveals the world as it truly is-
raw and wild and hateful and loving
the feeling of neurons connecting in ways
they've never connected before
your brain expanding in your very head
your love is the cool night air
leaves crunching underfoot
like when you bring your hands to your face
blow on them to warm them up
and they come away steamy
the shining moon above smiles down upon you
and the stars laugh
your love is driving down the highway at 1AM

street lamps fuzzy but glowing bright
an acoustic cover of your favorite song comes on the radio
and you hum along absentmindedly
fighting to stay awake
you've got to get home safe
because you know someone is there
and they're waiting for you
your love is the smell of old books
and the taste of warm apple cider
that feeling you get when you laugh so hard
you think you might be dreaming
your love is reflected on cool open waters
your love is moonlight

Out of the Blue
Emily Alice DeCicco

Love is meant
to take you unawares.
It strikes you.
Out of the blue,
like waking up midway
through Spring
and wondering when all
of this Earth had bloomed
in greens and endless
hues without your notice.

EZ Blackbird Pie
Henri Bensussen

High in the trees blackbirds
carouse, beaks to the cool
October wind, migrants escaping
stormy times in Oregon

Someday, next spring
I'll go there with them

me and the blackbirds

prancing the beaches
to catch the eye
of that special one

I'll spread my arms
embrace you for supper

Will you stay?

when they soar above
the plumey breakers
in courting couple batches

Dusky huckleberry lover
sweet, ripe, ready
my EZ blackbird pie

Fatal Attraction

Megha Sood

Fatal Attraction

That insatiable thirst
which rises from
the depths of my soul
and devours me
like a wild fire
this incessant need
to be wrapped
around your soul
like an unstoppable
contagion.

Megha Sood

Preference Over Judgement
HOKIS

Self love
Puppy love
First love
Unrequited love
Pining for first love, love
Pining for first love lost, love
Pining for the second love lost, love
Pining becomes love, love
I hear someone in every song, love
Addicted to love, love
Addicted to the novelty of falling into love, love
Promised love
Payoff for your dysfunctions, codependent love
Separated love
Divorced love
You cannot be who I need, projected anger, love
I cannot be who you need, projected shame, love
Trauma inoculated - fear of abandonment love
Trauma inoculated - I overshared, shameful and regretful, self-hate, and inch away from
love, kind of love
Pathological altruism, codependent as fuck love
Turn towards each other love
Turn away from each other love
Turn against each other love
Letting go of any love but self love, love
Forgiving, humble, deeply rooted in higher purpose love
Accepting you, just as you are, taking responsibility for myself love
Surrendering into my soul love
Love that never was, mind plays tricks, love
Love that never will be, star struck and seductive tendril, love
The universe sent you to teach me something love
Octopus momma,
starving to death, while staying with her eggs kind of love

SMITTEN

I will carry you if you sting my predators,
crab and anemone kind of love
I trust you to not eat me if I clean your teeth,
eel and shrimp kind of love
You will travel far on my back if you eat my ticks,
parallel path, buffalo and bird kind of love
I can pick you out of a crowd of look alikes, penguin love
I will wait by the shore each year, to dance, mate and
nest with only you, albatross kind of love
A pride of lions, communal love
I will wake you up, play with you, protect you,
and accept your scraps, grateful dog and depressed human kind of
love.
Doing the dishes love.
Making time love
Remembering details love
Friendship love
Holding space with open ears love
All of you is exactly what I love, love
I cannot handle all of you, compassionately stated, love
I cannot handle all of you, shamefully stated, projected anger, love
Orgy, what finger in what hole is irrelevant kind of love
Medicinal flesh kind of love
I adore the shape of my skin kind of self love
My body is but a vessel for love, love
Consensual, controlling sex kind of love
Powered sex, collapsing into vulnerability kind of love
Kissing only love
No kissing allowed love
When we kiss, fall into myself and be fully present with your fall
kind of love
Kill for you love
Depart so you can love, love
Letting you go love
Born of you love
Born of other love
Sibling love

This Is What Loves Looks Like

Favorite sibling love
Rather not have you as a sibling love
Parental contract love
Parent is my person love
Hold the hand of the passing love
I release you, love
Grieving love
Pain sparked growth self love, love
Falling into love, love
Rising into love, love
It's all rising because of love,
Love

I've a love
Sarah Vermillion

I've a love who crosses oceans
with her hair windswept, always in motion.
Her kisses sweet, her skin soaked in sunshine,
she's divine, and she's mine.
Scorpions in shots, she's done it
and sleep? She's never heard of it.
If the stars are up and shining, so is she.
Aruba and Jamaica, been there.
Volcanic mud, waterfalls, Bonaire;
she's crossed the world and there's so much to see,
but still she comes back to me.
And oh, if you could see it.
The way she looks at me.
Oh, the way I see it,
she's far away but never left me
I've a love whose smiles kill me
and the way she laughs will always thrill me.

Violets cast before we come

Candice Louisa Daquin

I always recognized your pain, a tender velvet touch beneath
though I would take it for my own
it suited your lonely eyes, the sad downturn of your mouth
for as some are drawn to laughter
I am attracted to souls of torment
the bar-flies and dusky persons, holding tight their sorrow
wishing to sail you to shore, salve your suffering
cup your bleeding in my hands
save you as I could not, save myself, from a chasing fate we all share
violets cast before we come
conspiring to swim ahead, slipping beneath water
dream of yesteryear, not so long ago
such a foolish urge and noble, to be protector, of broken things
yet seeing into you, I find the girl who sought such succor and I to give. all of my need
to love the unwanted, the tears, listing in the creases of your eyes
painting around the hurt, confuse the wolves, take your hand
it's how we stayed standing, when ground shook and revealed
we shared a split person, you one half of me
and I, reaching, climbing over, yawning space to get
closer to you

Portrait of Punishment
Rachel Finch

She is soft and willing,
her golden strands entwined
in my fingers and she is
telling me the story of how
courage became us.
I am hot and waiting,
drawing constellations in
the bruises on my thighs,
our portrait of punishment for
having pretty faces and heavy hips.
She tells me to recite the curse
of being born a pleasure to
greedy men and I kiss her
broken skin like the power of
the gods reside within my lips
and I can restore her.
She calls me Queen of Egypt and
whispers ancient witchcraft into
my mouth and I am already praying
the sorcery loves her through my hands.

Authentically Hers

Jack Neece

She is my authenticity
Truth flows from her fingertips and I drink
Before her I lived in shadows
Hidden behind curtains of shame and self-loathing
Whispers from my past haunted my passion
They stuck in my throat as if the words were my own
She taught me love and light while nurturing my dark
I was splintered and torn
I was ashamed and scared
My scars
A blanket I wrapped myself in to guard from further pain
Her touch
The soil my new seeds sprout in
Our limbs intertwine
I am in awe as my new flowers blossom

In the Harbour

Skye Myers

I brought you to the oyster bar where we slurped back the sea / and got drunk on the absinthe you'd snuck in, in a silver flask / we laughed with our heads thrown back as we ran out without paying the bill / our heavy boots beat against the wet sidewalk / our breath drifted into the night air like ghosts or our souls escaping / autumn, and holographic nights / black nail polish and clove cigarettes and when I kissed you, I tasted the empty hunger of you / I felt your desperate fingers at the nape of my neck and I wrapped you up in velvet / I held you too close, I think / you were like a baby bird ready to fly / and then you were gone like smoke or blood in the water / and all I could hear was your laughter / it's a pity we didn't see the warning signs blinking in neon / reflecting in the harbour

Does This Mean I Miss You?

Milena M. Gil

I'm in my car 15 minutes early for work
because I left early because I have anxiety
because I never felt good enough as a kid,
and I'm thinking about vegans and the one
time you went vegan for a month. And I'm
thinking about you going to Dunkin' Donuts
and not ordering anything, or maybe you
would take one of those "cheat days"
you were so fond of and get your usual—
unsweetened iced coffee with two pumps of
vanilla syrup and more milk than bean juice—
and there's no way I could know. And I'm
thinking about how thin your arms were, and
how my kisses would always bruise your pale,
translucent skin so easily, and maybe that's just
because you never got enough vitamins on
account of being a vegan, but you were only
vegan for about a month, so probably not

Minnie Mouse Dress
Kelsey Hontz

Remember, how Lou dared you to kiss me
Over the blare of the bass,
Thumping music sweet lava in our eardrums?
She translated for you, always forgetting
That I also spoke Spanish.
But when you leaned so close I flew
On the tips of your eyeliner wings
I forgot words in any language
And the thump transposed itself
Into the ventricles in my chest, so close to yours.

Soulmates
Marvlyn Vincent

With smoldering heat blazing in her eyes
And unbridled desires she could not disguise,
She recalled the very first time that they met
Two women in locker room
In the middle of the day,
Just before noon
She could not have imagined
Nor could she assume
One quick glance from a stranger
And the next moment
Her heart's in danger
She's heard stories
About this happening
One quick look and you go home pining
She could not let this go
From this stranger she wanted more
So much more than a quick glance,
Her mind conjures up, a quick romance
That happened by chance
With this thought in her head,
And consumed by something,
For the first time that was not dread
She left her home,
Determined to find this woman,
For this feeling she must own,
Now back in her sanctuary, in her home
A bright future up ahead,
With paths unknown
They hold on to the present
Embracing each other
With no dreams or plans or hopes to smolder
The desire galloping and running rampant
For what they found in each other's arms
They are unrepentant.

Is A Seascape Ever Enough
Lindz McLeod

White-knuckled on the tiller; the water is
so calm. All the captaincy is inside me,
storm-flecked and tightlipped,
bucking through the waves.
Listen. Hear that? These tides are you,
the girl who breathes the stars.
Until the end of days,
past the trumpets and the
judgement.
Carved by hand.
Surely the crown gets all the keys; those chambers
and dungeons inside myself
locked and locked again. For my safety
and yours.
Cede control of the
path to the gallows;
I swing open at the close.
This is the fault along the horizon;
the land is yours, to plough how you want it.
Tilled to the north, until I swerve,
ox bowed soil slanting right. Come with
me, pack your bag. Leave your shadow to
disappear into the sunrise with eyes
shading regret-grey,
all the honeyed paths we
can make up.
Unhurried.
The woman on the pier, the fortune teller,
pushing back her chair and asking you
plainly, so boldly - what were you so afraid of?
Ashes, I'd say.
Ashes and endings.
A kingdom so very familiar with that look.

First Kiss
Sarah Karowski

I'm realizing that it's normal for twelve-year-old girls
to kiss each other. sleepover weekends turned
exploration, finding out how our bodies worked—
but seeing you with a boy hurt worse
than when my parents fought. & when you kissed
his cheek, that was the first time I felt invisible.
when you held his hand, I hated him.
so, it really was fireworks, that night, tucked away from
our friends, rigid on that foreign mattress. when you
kissed me it was sweet, like tangerine,
like the bubblegum we'd share, like the movies,
& I know that twelve-year-olds just do this sort of thing,
but your saliva on my lips was an open door, a realization:
alike more than like, like when Lizzie kissed Gordo,
my smile strained cheeks: vindication—
I bet he doesn't know how you taste

but, twelve-year-olds do this all the time.
at school that Monday, you were holding his hand
& that's the first time I felt slow motion.
tightly folded note just for me: you said experimenting.
twelve-year-old girls don't fall in love with their best friends.
you had feelings for him, & maybe me, but that wasn't true.
you held his hand over the lunch room table,
& held mine under it. later that week, I heard
you kissed him. for the first time.
your first kiss.
how special.

a stór

Lindz McLeod

You will walk into the sea,
it won't matter where or when.
I am the wilder horses of the foam—
who can say which one of us
will ride the other,
Acushla
and response;
hold my head under,
tugged like seawrack,
réalta eolais.

Down, down and swallow
between your shoreline limbs
until the night can lift us up.
Gifted the sound of conches
held against your cheek for years,
hearing the sirens sing of
myths to come

blue honey
Dani Bowes

i met you when you had aqua tips
and we sat awkwardly
around a table
i told my ex how i was intimidated
by the way you felt so cool
so effortless,
when i really met you -
your hair was brown
and i smoothed it
over your forehead
on the corner of the couch
this was the first time i ever saw you cry.
i was scared my hands might sting
like the tears on your throat
but we stayed there in the stillness,
anyway, we stayed there, sitting,
waiting for spring.

Epilogue
T. M. Servin

I didn't know I was capable
of loving her that way.
This one, that wore her smallness
like an irreversible condition
on her skin.
She was seemingly frail, and
quietly cunning,
but to me, beautiful.

(She was my first Her.)

I didn't know that in our
seasoned years there were still
trophies to be had,
or that I could be one.

(She was my first Her.)

Seemingly frail, and wearing small,
but strong enough
to watch me stumble,
to watch me break,
to watch me try to find my way
after,
blinded by the glare of her victory.

(She was my first Her.)

The thing I'll always remember most
was her smile as she
placed my soul upon her mantle,
that secret smile that beguiles so
many,
because only she and I know

just how good she is
at wearing small,
at seeming frail.

a history of femmes
Tekla Taylor

I like full skirts best when I sit unladylike,
Skirts up in a froth around my thighs,
My knees at saucy angles. I love the plural,
"skirts." layers: petticoats and mystery
and lace.
in long skirts in the snow I am Jo March,
Fearless
and warm. in summer i am
floating fairy queen. i might welcome
some caressing hand or slap it. Full-skirted,
caprice is my birthright. I am frivolous and flouncing,
I am busy.
I am a flower. Above all, and precious,
I am delightful to old women,
to those who miss the silhouettes of youth.

Losing Me by Loving You

T. M. Servin

I try not to listen to it:
the haunting melody of you.
Sometimes though,
I'll still put it on.
As the strings come together
and fingers gently caress piano keys,
you return.

This always makes me think of you.
Sometimes it still brings tears,
the loss of me,
before I ever knew,
I could love the lilt of a woman's voice
calling my name.

Oh, I was innocent,
and naïve,
and now,
how I wander…

Guardian

Sarah Kacala

They tell me it's wrong. That she, is wrong, and that I am wrong, because I love her. But who are THEY? They know nothing about me. They cannot cradle my fears, or crawl beneath my veins. They cannot feel the silence within my tears, or hold these scars that still remain. They don't live inside this skin of mine. And I guess for so many years; neither did I. I didn't wake up one day, and decide that I was gay. For I know now, that I was born this way. It's who I was meant to be, from the very first breath this life gave me. I stumbled in the dark for so much of my life, that even in my most authentic moments, I could scarcely handle the light.

Closeted and afraid is where I remained, until one day I woke up, and I didn't feel the weight. I didn't feel the same as I had always felt before. I stood up on my feet, I turned the handle, and I opened up the door. Never to return again; I was in that cage no more. It was time to be true to who I am. No more living my life, in that closet on the floor. I leapt into the light not prepared for the fight, and it left me there bleeding alone. But being who I am and knowing where I stand, meant more to me than fake religious friends, and the four walls and the ceiling that I had always called my home.

I wandered around aimless and lost, until I found her. She quickly became my everything; my peace, inside the hurricane. The winds were swirling all around me. But as long as she was with me, I was safe. As long as she stood there by my side, I remained unshakeable, and unafraid. She held my hand, and my whole world changed. Her laughter and her smile brightened up my darkest of days. She made it all worth it; all of the loneliness. All of those years holding onto my secret, as I stumbled in that tiny closet in the dark. All those years of tripping over my own damn feelings, as I tried so desperately, to turn off my heart; to shut down forever, it's innermost parts.

She lit me up, and held me close. And in this chaotic world, to me she matters most. She is my guardian. She is the protector of my soul.

She gave me her hand and her heart, to hold. This earthborn human savior, whom I've come to love and cherish; whom I've come to know so well. She spun magic, into my nightmares. She made heaven, out of my hell.

On the Eve of my Birthday

Olivia Chachinsky

If there is just enough time in the last few moments
before I turn nineteen, I would like to dance with you,
perhaps in the soft blue light of your dad's projector.
Your hand will press gently into the small of my back

as my adolescence crumbles into the cobalt of crushed
butterfly wings and dried grass and an expanse
of sky that stands bold in the face of Time.

In a few minutes, I will no longer be the girl you fell
in love with, but a full-grown woman. My eyes will widen unafraid,
and I will no longer be in love with you because suddenly I will know
better.

We will sway in that soft blue light, and I will listen to your heart
beat a reveille, and all that is unsaid between us will melt
away into the night air. As we part, and I dive into a sky
of stars, I will be nineteen, and love everything that is not you.

Letters to my love

Susan M. Conway

It is a curious thing, my love, the bitter taste the heteros have for our right to choose who we love, how we love, and what we do with our bodies. I just want to waltz right up to every intolerant prick and be like, "Get off my areola." And then you and I, we would walk away, arm in arm, laughing and laughing.

Let's make plans to do that one day soon.

To me, I care that they are toxic and hurt people with their toxicity, but in regard to you and me, I don’t care what they say as long as you still believe in US with me; as long as our love will forever taste like strawberry Fanta, and warm summer evenings in bed, watching The Craft like it's the first time, for the millionth time.

You are my favorite person.

I love you loudly, intentionally, eyes wide open, and a heart full of FUCK YES.

Mass for the heathens
Jesica Nodarse

She says I am her church
But she...
She is the god that dwells within

june night opera

Tekla Taylor

a cricket quartet played the sun down,
and I
cannot stop thinking of you. a bullfrog baritone,
owl prima donna
take the stage.
now the treetops heap soft black against the blue
the porch is spot lit; I am blind to stars.
should I be fearless now and step offstage,
sink ankle deep to fragrant grass and let my eyes expand?

i am
not yet insensible to hoot-owl
arias nor
soft and falling dusky Junes
nor thoughts of you like high and silent cries
like bats or stagehands constant flicker,
black wings against a sable sky.

It Took a Mere Glance
Renee Furlow

Karaoke Night with Lady Rose and Babe
Kindra M. Austin

Cigarette smoke hangin' heavy, an artist's veil, muffles the bar lights; and
I feel marvelous amidst a pall of my own making. This is my scene: Karaoke,
Friday night with Rose and Babe. Rose is singin' Janis Joplin—
Me and Bobby McGee.
Lordy, can that Lady scream.

And kiss.
Rose kissed me on the lips, once,
just because she'd felt like it. I was drunk on gin and tonic.
I've prized her ever since, in my silent way.

Behind a smoke screen:
The lovers are dancing now, two mystics converging.
Someone's weaving words into the microphone—
I Put a Spell On You.

Oh,
I'd forgotten for a moment that I'm the one singing,
so entranced am I by Lady Rose and Babe.
I Put a Spell On You.

Oh,
I'd forgotten for a holy moment...
the spell's been cast on me, and
this is what love looks like.

Skin to skin,
sandalwood fragrant, and beaded with sweat.
Breasts to breasts.
Hips to hips.
I watch these women
root themselves

deep
into the floor.
They intertwine their willow limbs, and
I feel marvelous
because
this is what love looks like.

Someday I'll Love Maria Gray

after Ocean Vuong

Maria Gray

Maria,
train your eyes on the planes,
the chemical trails, the wrecks
plummeting through a thousand feet
of cold and useless sky. Drain the mouths
you've met, gaping and open
as a wound. Step over the canyons wrapped
in gauze. Consider the bridges you've jumped from
and all the times I've caught you. Call to mind
the water. How it looks unbroken.
Maria, I don't need to tell you
what it's all about. Sea breaking on the rocks.
Paint peels away from the wall
to which it owes itself.
His fingers pass through you
like a fishhook — there will be life afterwards,
if you are smart. Maria, be smart.
The mist clears where it meets the mountains
and always, somewhere, someone chips away at something
unfathomable. A feather brushes against the coal
every thousand years. Motionless old friends
collect flies in the kitchen. Here is the sugar bowl.
Here is the cinnamon. Here is the toast
you forgot to eat. The fibers of sweet fruits
make homes between your teeth.
Like the dinosaurs, our bodies
pull us closer to extinction. I, the spine-backed
stegosaurus; you, the meteor
hurtling towards my head. Whatever I am now,
I owe it to you. Whatever I am now,
grief remains the mortar. You, the bricks.
You, raised above my head

Go Figure
Jennifer Mathews

had she ever gotten that bizarre feeling
right above her stomach
when she saw a girl friend

i had asked her in eighth grade

she said no
and that was that

remembering
Tekla Taylor

i remember that
short white dress blazed pure in the sun,
the skirt flared out like a corona
by the fountain, that day. i almost didn't see you,
i was blinded, bright blue sky and thousand-watt
sunlight
and that white dress refracted
everything. when we hugged your body was warm, you were
laughing. you were light, and
heat
your hair smelled like hibiscus and your skin looked just
like
honey
dressed in white like morning-glories.
we talked
a little but I wish I'd stayed.
now i feel you strongest and I miss you more than ever
on those brightest, cloudless,
hottest blue-white days.

Another Ode to Sara
Kelly-Girl Johnston

I remember the photograph clearly,
            it was black and white
with a spectrum of grays.

Your figure,
            it was overwhelming, honestly,
you had positioned
                                                        your figure…

At this point we were young
            —very young—
sexting was not nearly a thing!

Folks could still find
            broad patches of quiet
to nuzzle into together, or solitary.

We had found such
             a patch of suspended quiet
and, floating there

You positioned your figure
            in the black and white
and infinite spectrum of grays.

You showed me light.

Quick, Think of Something
Georgia Park

It's a cheerful sunset
through the luxurious floor-to-ceiling windows
of my temporary office
featuring golden bursts of blue
the same hues of a parakeet
I once attached sentimentality to

I hold myself, watching
and remember that once
I loved well and was cherished

I hold myself knowing
I can't get that back again
I grant, maybe that's enough
for one lifetime—maybe it's time
to wish for something different

I cajole myself into daydreaming
while the light still warms my cheek
ok, so what's the next great thing?

someday, I think
I'd like to leave
this little carnival city
I'd miss my friends
but I think that, someday
I should do it

or maybe, maybe…
she'll come back to me
then, of course
everything would be different-

I'd want different things

or maybe, maybe…

the sun sets
I leave the office
I come back again
repeat the sunset

The Palm

P. M. Houghton-Harjo

My fingers sink into garden dirt,
soft coolness covering the skin cracks.

"Is this was what it is like to cut someone up, and reach in?"
I ask my mother,

"Is this—?"
Her eyes look up, laughing.

She can lift up the world's skin as easily as a surgeon,
grasp soft, wet organs, and

plant something living by the corpses she created.
She has always been good at creating.

The soil always makes my hands dry;

I push them further in to make my palms rougher and rougher.
I pick my hand up,

palm to the sky, dirt in the deep grooves of my skin
(I am getting older).

My love line is long.

My life line is short.

Regret becomes a worm in the high pit of my chest—
I know that I haven't looked at my lover's palm long enough.

I have looked at the base of her thumb.
The tip of her index.
Short nails, never painted.

SMITTEN

I have looked at every mesa I have kissed before,
    but not the length of her love line.
    not at the height of her Jupiter's mount.

The garden makes me promise things
    (as if I am in the presence of a God—a creator—Mother
Fuckin' Earth Herself). So,

I promise the redbudblood dirt in my hands that I will look longer,
    at the length of the valleys in my girl's Oklahoma mountain
    hand.

Missing U
Katharine Love

I miss the u that was part of us.
I miss saying
"*I'll have to ask my girlfriend*"
before committing us to
any social engagements.
I miss late night
after date night kisses.
I miss your hand that you
placed always so gently on
the small of my back.
I miss your cat that slept
on my side of our bed.
I miss your raucous laugh
that annoyed movie goers
and opera patrons but gave
me the courage to live
my life loud.
I miss licking the juice
off your fingers
from the plums that we
shared in the morning
after making love all
night long.
I miss calling you from
the train to let you know
I'll be home at eleven
not at nine, because the
train broke down
in the middle of nowhere,
but we are all safe and I can't wait
until I'm with you again.

I miss the u that was
part of us.

The History of the Invert
Didi Artier

I had a calling once

slathered thickly on my chest like *Olbus Oil* when the flu threatens to shut you in with powdered cough

straining to come out, this heaviness, a confession need not, still strove to speak her rainbow tongue

I am a lesbian I am proud

in the Winter time, people spent great care bundling their throats and noses against arctic draft

in the Summer-time, people labored over deep tan lines and perpetual look of bright light

they did not care who I was, or why

but my sisters, they did, the ones who stood at the entrance to the lesbian bars I ventured into with trepidation

giving me side-ways glances, disapproving stares, the dislike and approbation of a different species

sitting at the bar, ordering a watered-down version, trying to make conversation felt harder than cold or heat

wet or dry, hands pushing me into a corner were metaphysical but felt every bit as exclusionary as

if I were among enemies

had I asked; *why do you cast me out, what is the cause of your unfriendliness?* They may have come out and said it *you are not one of us*

you are not a real lesbian

and let it hang like the music swelling on many colored arms and shoulders lifting up to join in a common dance

you are not welcome

I left the bar feeling as if I had worn a Scarlet letter or perhaps stumbled into the wrong place drunk and

shame-faced I entered an Italian restaurant and ordered a coffee, sitting there it felt less hateful than

among my own kind

hearing words whispered into my back like hot knives, words can hurt as much as actual steel I know this now

you are just a sight-seer

nothing about you is queer

are you a weekend bisexual or a lost lipstick femme?

the taunts needled me and I wanted to return and somehow prove I was every bit their equal

just like a black woman is told, you are too dark Chica, you are too light mama, your color doesn't fit

our prescription or notion of what it means to be B.L.A.C.K. or of color

gentle exclusion or violent, what does it matter? The same sense of not belonging permeates your soul

if you cannot hang with your people, where do you have to go? I
woke up with a hangover and next to a man who

told me I had picked him up in a bar in Soho barely able to stand, he
was sorry for me and took me to his apartment

but I did not touch you

my clothes were on, I smelt of beer and cigarettes and the stink of
something deeper, a foul scent of not belonging

a part of me wished I had been sober enough to say to the young man;
go on then, do your best, I no longer care

for labels or truth

such was my breakage and the feeling of exile, sometimes you hurt
yourself when others do and there is nothing left

I walked along the river, mascara run and tears wetting the dry salt
white

men who were crabbing, waved meaty arms from the river's edge

gold statues on the bridge, were of women entwined and I recalled
seeing a lesbian couple in a film once

who did not pretend to be men or hate other women who were women

my desire for a woman did not come with a detailed description, just
be female and kind

I had omitted the part where all the places to meet women were
barred to

girls like me who didn't fit a stereotype

and this, before the internet, so no girls, aside the ones in my imagination

who called on me in the evening with bright smiles and lovely silk dresses

I ended up marrying a man a few years later out of loneliness and not feeling

I could be a lesbian if the code included shaving your hair, dressing in men's clothes and

shaming single women who dared

to seek love

it didn't last very long, I am bad at pretending to be; someone I am not

so, the whole world was closed to me

I stood alone, twenty years til a shift in thinking brought

young women out who held each other's hands and some had long hair and painted their nails and wore espadrilles

by then, I was grey and bitten down by disappointment

I could only sit and watch like I had many years past

without the words to describe my pain

to youths with happy faces, never knowing the

history of the invert

After the Reading
Carol H. Jewell

After the reading
I walked on Lark toward where I'd parked,
saw people sitting on
their stoops.
Walked up Lancaster,
looking at a house that had
a room at the back,
with two walls of glass,
beautiful windows.
I didn't stop looking until,
"Ma'am, is anything wrong?"

"No, why do you ask?"

"You were staring at me!"

"No, actually, I was looking at that pretty house."

I walked further, only a block from the truck, now,
hard, behind me, in the distance, heard,
"I ain't no lesbian!"

Well. I am. But
that doesn't mean anything;
I was looking at a house!

Just Saying

Carolyn Martin

This morning
you never stopped.
Of course
I wanted to hear
every detail about
yesterday's barbeque
in your old neighborhood
and who married whom
and the history of their kids
and how your childhood tribe
crept across
the grouchy neighbor's yard
on sulky summer nights.

I was also intrigued
by the Kennedy conspiracy,
how magnesium
is essential for the brain,
and why I should avoid
every wheat-filled thing.

I almost snuck in
Thích Nhất Hạnh's
The bread we eat
is the whole cosmos

but his words got lost
in the orbit of your voice
along with gardenia blooms,
my latest poem,
and the stream of clouds
easing from the coast.

In case you're interested,

SMITTEN

I’ve bookmarked these
along with the truth
that announced itself
in a waking dream:
we are dipoles
magnetized steadily.

Meet me for a chat
on the patio tonight.
Perhaps you’ll acquiesce
when I quote John Donne:
For God sake hold
your tongue and let me love.

Butch-ish
Paula Jellis

I like three-piece suits
and I don't love sports
but I loved Martina
on the courts

I love to tango and I love to dance
I like holding hands
and I love romance
I love long dresses
and I like short hems
and I'm here to say:
I love the Femmes
I'm Butch-ish, I'm Butch-ish
I'm not a Broadway baby
I'm a Broadway Dyke!
and I'll tell you what I like
Women.... in tech
Women....on the stage
Women....writing plays
From Aphra Behn to Carolyn Gage!

Angelou, Baum, Carroll, Chambers, Childress, Churchill, Clinton,
Ensler, Glancy, Hansberry, Hellman,
Hughes, Kapil, Kron, Miguel, Oliva, Sanchez, Shange, Shaw, Split
Britches, Vogel, Walker, Wasserstein, West,
5 Lesbian Brothers...Bechdel, Chin!
I love women who love to flirt
or are in the White House
or are digging in dirt
I love libraries and I love to read,
I'm built for comfort, not built for speed
I've got short hair
and I've got short nails
and if you'd like

some more details
come up and see me
come up and see me
come up and see me
sometime
Because....I'm...
Butch-ish

Moving Day
Kim Harvey

There we are surrounded by boxes, piles of photographs, papers stacked. One
Hurried, half-assed toast to open hearts and wet mouths, and we'll be
Eating take-out, sprawled on your living room floor. I can't stop looking over

To watch you look around at everything: in the corner, the books you'll give away.
How much time does it take to decide what's worth holding?
It all happens in a moment, and then it's the moments you can't let go.
Notebooks full of them, all those words, and not one that works, not one
Good verb to tell you what it's like to pack away the life we never had as you
Show me insta-prints of a passionate kiss in a photo booth, girls pressed together

In twos, one of them always you, you holding someone else's hand. Come

Monday, you're moving in with your girlfriend and it's time I went home to mine. It's easy
Enough to see why I let you in back then, why you took root even as I pushed you
Away. And whatever it was you felt for me, it wasn't love you've said; whatever it was, it was
Not for keeps, won't fit neatly in a shoe-box labeled with one-word possessives
That say hers, mine, ours. In some other world, we may have a house where I fall freely

To sleep in your arms. Here, we're nothing more than dangling modifiers, past participles, parts

Of speech that will never be contained in a spoken sentence. So you won't
Say, *This box is for the sex we didn't have*, as you tear off the packing tape and put it

Aside, our empty crate of impossibilities. But I know you. I know just how
You'll watch me take the things I meant to say when I leave with the throwaways

Obsession #1

Christine E. Ray

Me, unable to stop thinking about you
You, the one I couldn't have
Push-me, pull-you
Come closer
Go away
Me, always off-balance
You, one minute cold, the next tender
An elaborate dance
Taking turns leading
Me, always wanting
You, always inscrutable
Maybe you did just value my friendship
Maybe I was a challenge
Maybe you just wanted to get laid
I wanted to climb into your skin
Wrap myself around your heart
Fuse onto your soul
Ease that haunted look in your eyes
Be the one you couldn't breathe without
Maybe you were wise to keep the distance
Me, endless need
You, my weapon of self-destruction

I Keep Looking for You

Nayana Nair

I am floating towards you
against my own will.
I struggle and lose
against my fate,
against what my heart loves.
I am floating in your eyes in
spite of all my flaws.
I am happy that
you love me.

I am floating again
floating away from you.
and my heart has forgotten
the love I had for you. But
I fear
somewhere in me, you are still there
hiding in places I won't look.
I keep looking from you
So, I can be free from you
I keep looking for you
Even when I don't want you.

In my sleep
I open a door to another dream
where I drift in an endless ocean
Wearing the clothes, I wore on a school trip
on a boat that capsized, on a show I saw long ago.
As I lay blinded by sun, by hunger, by life
I uttered your name, again and again
as if you would answer.
Your name was the only happiness in that world.
Your name was my only sorrow.

The Mask
A. Staley

A mask covered my face
It used to protect me
I thought it protected me
I became the mask
I couldn't live without it
I am the mask now
Then I met you
You started to chip away at the corners
Vulnerability is scary as hell
Who am I without my mask?
Can I live without it?
Can I love without it?
You… YOU finally broke my mask
Your vulnerability showed me love
You showed me strength and patience
My mask is gone…
It will never return
YOUR love is my new mask
You helped create the new me.

For She is Beauty
Candice Louisa Daquin

If her heart were a drum
it would be outlawed for beating too loud
for the insistent and unwary pound
keeping wakeful when those who rest, wish for silence
beneath her a lake of feeling
if a mime enacted, his black cloth fingers, would grow numb with gesticulation
her wordless passion smacked into taut skin
trembling at the imagining of her proximity
she breaks a sweat on the fine hair of her neck
a necklace of pearl and moonstone
for each sway of her fruiting body, she is the picker of her sanity
a welcome devil in empty playground
she blinks into darkness, seeing futures;
in one, she is swimming in dark water, illuminating only her want
reaching shore, she searches for her among shadows
trying to imagine the way she feels, naked and shaking off
the spill of her longing
in another they are talking; far into time and beyond, where
landscapes break open pink and ochre, like food consumed by gods
she cannot yet tear herself away, from the smoothness of her skin
or how her cheeks slope like arching cats, pulling beauty from places she didn't know existed
she is a terrifying girl who knows her power and still, is lost at times to its art
the wince and crimp of her slimness, like a willow tree, capturing storms
she holds her head like a wave, cresting against soft shoreline
proud and a little self-assured, the quivering arrow of her curves
tied like a bow around desire, burns in its simplicity
her skin is mango and sunlight, of all her lives spent, before she was found
still like a water fountain, just before it bursts, released from clay
there is harmony and music in her tread and no one yet

has found the riddle to her heart
something distant and wafer thin, like a fabric of unknown origin
it is not her wish to change anything, but the temperature she feels
when they press against the other, beneath roar of blood and live wire
crackling into couplets of lightning
it is not her wish to alter one second, save the moment she relents and
sensing something good, releases her perfume and all the capture of
her loveliness
till they mingle as one energy, burning their quickening on the tail of
some unearthed connection, where beneath the moon they
reach for each other and not, the solace of being alone
lying in a circle like warm pleats, she draws her hand slowly
over the silk of her, without words sufficient
holds her breath, as long as it can stay
spellbound by her presence, the entire world paused
in reflecting pools, oceans, never deep enough to swallow
the intensity of her regard
for she is beauty.

I Begin With the Exclamation Point Because This Fact About You Makes Me Laugh

P. M. Houghton-Harjo

You don't like peaches!
"It's a texture thing", you say,
even though I already know
(I only offer because I love you,
and I want to offer you everything).
So I wait for the peach juice on my fingertips to dry
(and wipe the rest of the soft yellow sap on my nice jeans)
before I place them at the intersection of your hair and neck.
(There, it feels like peach skin and I want to tell you this small irony).
This is the cue for you to kiss me, soft and with a smile,
and you do.
I hope that you can taste the leftovers because
you deserve to taste something sweet
(like you are to me).

An Unassuming Playdate
Sonia Beauchamp

The beige of her blouse is the same
as my living room carpet
minus the stains of spilt sippy cups and dirty feet.

Modest beige fails to hide breasts
swimming under waves of creamed silk
and the faint smell of spoiled milk.

The sash that's knotted beside her throat
does nothing except ask
for her high-collared neckline to become

undone.

Previously published in *Screen Door Review*, Issue 6, June 15, 2019.

Nakedness
Wil Staley

Last night, in my most vulnerable state;
my despair and pain, I chose you.
As I lay near, I gave you my body.
Covering nothing up, all of me became yours.
Yes, I have given myself to you many times before,
but never while my soul allowed my fear to drop to the floor;
unclothing my skin in the brightest light for you to adore.
You completely broke me in the most beautiful way
and I will never be the same.
That's the point, my love, it was you
who took away my shame.

Forever
Amie Campbell

I want to say that I will love you forever
But our time on this earth is limited
And we do not have forever to love one another
If we had forever, I would love you a little more every day
I would plant a rose bush every spring
And leave a flower on your pillow every night
If we had forever, I would count the hairs on your head
And smile as each one turned gray
I would learn how to make your favorite cake and bake it every Sunday
Until I knew the recipe by heart
If we had forever, I would wait to hold your hand on a snowy winter day
I wouldn't kiss you until the third date
And we could take years to learn each other's bodies
But we don't have forever
Our days are numbered
Our time is measured
And we just don't know when it will run out yet
So, I will love you with the ferocity of a gladiator fighting to his death
Kicking and screaming and clawing for every second I can have with you
Struggling through pain and fear just to keep you near to me

Masterpiece
Sarah Vermillion

She outdoes the Mona Lisa with her sweet, contagious smile,
and an odalisque by Delacroix wouldn't even be worthwhile.
Somehow Edward Hopper's sunlight, pulling dusk across the world,
is nothing close to perfect when up against this girl.
Van Gogh's "Starry Night" can't come close to her dark eyes.
Even Escher's twisted staircase can't match these butterflies.
And the awe-inspiring landscapes painted masterfully by Monet
can't get my recognition when this girl looks my way.
It's nothing you can fathom. It cannot be controlled.
No brush nor pen can capture the girl with the breathtaking soul.

Anatomy of a Heartbreak

Tan Shivers

"I can't do this anymore", she wrestled the words from her lips
My feet went numb. The same feet
that took late night walks with her
on the beach during those cool
summer nights
My legs felt as stiff as the oak
trees we scurried under to find shelter
from the pop-up Charleston rain showers
on our occasional walk through the park
My knees buckled like the old makeshift
bridge we crossed while trekking across the
pond to our secret hideout. Each step felt as
dangerous as our love, but still worth the risk
My thighs burned like the bonfires we watched
as we sat camp side with friends. No matter
where she sat in our little group, she'd always
end up in my lap; it was her favorite place to sit
My stomach knotted like the old rope we used
to tie around a worn-out tire, we found in the back
of her uncle's red pickup truck. We hung it on a
tree on his farm and made a charming little swing
My hands tingled like my tongue after being
forced to consume the worst sour candy as payment
for losing a friendly bet. She'd always laugh at
the silly faces I made as I tried to brave the tartness
My arms felt as heavy as the bulky, sun beaten
wicker baskets I carried after we spent the majority
of a mid-July afternoon picking peaches. She'd always
try to convince me there was room for one more peach
My chest sunk like the coins she'd gleefully toss into the
wishing well at the mall. She'd close her eyes so tight, it
made her forehead wrinkle a little. After letting out a sigh,
she'd release the coins as if releasing doves into the sky
My neck tightened like the chain on her bicycle after

having to repair it for the millionth time. I always felt like a
surgeon performing a critical operation the way she'd study
my hands as I carefully affixed the metal chain back to its proper
place
My mouth was dry like the air on those cold winter mornings
we spent cuddled in our warm bed hoping the alarm clock
had somehow made a mistake by ringing too early ahead
of its designated time. We took turns hitting the snooze button
My nose felt congested like the traffic after a baseball game at
the Joe Riley stadium. I found her frustration with the sluggish
pace of the cars to be considerably entertaining. I'd jokingly
keep track of the number of times she'd yell, "Just drive, people!"
My ears rang like the cowbells she'd playfully clank
to summon me to the kitchen table to partake in one of
her masterfully crafted meals. The more I pretended
not to hear it, the louder she'd clang them together
My eyes filled with tears like the ones that trickled
down her face after engaging in a nuclear war of words.
My arsenal consisted of the most hurtful things I could
think of and, sadly, I used them without hesitation
My heart broke just like hers after I'd selfishly shatter one
of many promises, never realizing the pain it caused her.
She'd tirelessly try to explain the physical distress each heartbreak
produced but I never quite understood it... until now

On Leaving Iran
Rebecca Ruth Gould

The plane ascends.
Women disrobe,
crossing into Turkey's airspace.
Their hair cascades like waterfalls.
I lift my skirt to let my
legs breathe.
So much sin is compressed
between my teeth & my toes!
The wind caresses my hair.
The carpet's threads bend beneath my feet.
I am happy to unveil
—
for myself, not a male guardian
—
to return to my body,
to desire myself for myself,
in this corner
of the cockpit
poised between two countries,
without male eyes
watching over me.

Finding Home
Samantha Renee

Hello, there you are,
I have been waiting for my whole life to meet you.
I'm sorry I can't speak.
Or am I talking too much?
The weather is cold, wet, and gray.
We are sweaty, covered in mud, with red noses.
You smile with your eyes before your mouth even moves.
I can't stop staring.
Summer nights spent beneath the stars,
nature's symphony playing in the background.
Your soft hands holding mine in the dark.
It wasn't safe in the light.
I fit just beneath your chin where I could breathe your intoxicating scent.
While your hands ran through my hair.
You opened my eyes to the laughter that surrounded me.
It was yours.
A perfect childlike girl giggle that didn't hold back.
You helped me see the softer side of things.
You took my hand and guided me out of my darkness.
You showed me love.
I felt our souls light up, and peace fill my body.
No words needed or could explain this moment.
The world is new, the future magic.
I was home.

Love, Not Hate
Destiny Killian

You'd hate me if you knew me
You all would
I'm the one you hide your children from,
the one who invades your sacred spaces
I hide behind closet doors,
afraid of what's outside, looking in
Am I the monster they made me
or are they the monsters
for condemning me
If we are all sinners,
then who's to say my sin
is worse than yours
Who's to say it's a sin at all
when it comes from the heart
Could it be my heart is corrupt
Is it in my soul
Maybe it's in my brain
There must be something wrong with me
if you all say so
It must be some unknown disease
since you all want to cure me
I didn't ask for this
I didn't choose to be this way
I only asked for love
and the freedom to love
So please
No more hate.

Memory Beaches
Tara Caribou

my lips sigh as the water slowly slips
through black grains of sand
how I long to feel your caress
even as the waves gently lap my feet
your red lips quivered
when my thumb stroked you there
an intake of breath and
your eyes sparkled before softly closing
I remember your quiet hum of contentment
for I had placed this special moment
within my breast for the future
I miss your kisses
just like I miss my hand on your hip
back then girls weren’t meant to love girls
just like now
and you’re long gone from me
every so often
I pull out your memory
and smile tears of wistful yearning

How you see me as androgynously styled
Dr. Sneha Rooh

And I argue how I'm hell bent on femme.
How top I actually am you mention
I stare at you for saying that
You smile and say "it's true"
I agree, "I am changing stereotypes" I say
Someone talks to me and how you stay
Though your drink is empty.
Slowly your hands are on my shoulder
I smile at the signal
The person doesn't talk about the same thing more.
They leave and we go to get us a drink
Hearts have electromagnetic waves I realise,
People at the institute of heart math were right.
You talk about static electricity
And I am thinking of telepathy
You hold my hand and it's confirmed
We walk out, walk around
Talk some more
It’s late in the evening now
You finally ask me if you can call me
I say I am not sure I’ll have something to talk about every day.
"You already decided every day?" You ask
For the first time I feel I’m bad at the game.

A Letter to Jane

Olivia Chachinsky

Jane, I have looked
for you in all the places
you could possibly be found,
yet you have evaded
me. You hide in plain sight—
you drift into thin air and float,
silent and unforgiving, above my head.
I have wished on countless stars
that you would return to me and lie
on my sunburnt chest,
that you would cry
for me from the deepest
chambers of your beating heart,
yet you say and see nothing.
Jane, I have tried to love you with all that is within me,
but all I can muster is two lotus seeds
and a loaf of rye bread. When the blackberries
fall from their green prisons,
and the Indian sun dives
below the welcoming horizon,
I'll sit alone with the beasts
and feel your absence
and I will try again.

Crazy
Susie Fought

She's standing up there. Stiff. One leg throbbing. Holding the microphone like a baby bird. Back lit. Blue neon. Large afro loose curls in silhouette. Cigarette smoke thick, softens your heart. Her hips start to sway softly. Electric guitar cuts right through this smoke and melts your limbs. You begin to rock there on your bar stool.

The blue. Her hair. The guitar. They all melt away and you're dancing now in Sandy's back yard. Someone put the radio in the window and turned the volume up. Mick Jagger's sweltering voice. Wild, wild horses. You're spinning in the leaves. Barefoot. Sandy bumps into you. And just like that you're slow dancing. Just like at the Junior High dances. Your brother does the light shows. He lets you sneak in to watch. Live bands. You thought they were famous. But they were just a bunch of high school kids.

You like the slow dancing best. It looks real. It looks like love. It looks like something important.

She stops singing. The guitar goes quiet. Nobody claps. It's just some bar on 2nd street. You can hear the chattering now the music stopped. You look around the bar for her. She must be on break. You wish you were the kind of person who could walk right up to her and say, 'hey, nice song'. But you know you won't.

Maybe if she stands at the bar next to you. Maybe if she lingers, waiting for her free beer. Maybe then you'd get up the nerve to say something. But she's gone.

Probably off home to her boyfriend. Or uptown to another gig. Doesn't matter.

You'll never see her again.

Sex, Suddenly, Everywhere
Jessica Jacobs

In shop class, that redhead with the jumpsuit zippered
from throat to crotch, trilling, *Boys, don't touch my zipper*,
until they trailed her like goslings, transfixed
by the shiny metal pull. The couple caught
naked in the science building bathroom. Backhand
whispers of *But I wouldn't even take my shoes off in there!* And how
many
eighth-grade dance parties in a country club boathouse, some girl
in the corner crying about some boy, some boy nervously plucking
the wales of his corduroys, waves lapping
—unheard but always lapping— as I got freaked by the Pagan twins
to a *Boys II Men* slow jam.
Confused girl meshed between two confused brothers, I tried not to
stare
at the girls I wished against me instead.
∞
And every day those hallways: crowded cattle shoots, musked up
clusters of young bodies, slap of sandals, snap of bra straps, high
sweet
stench of mall-bought perfume. My nose to the back of another girl's
neck, close enough to see a single strand, escaped, curling beneath
her collar, the gym class dampness between her shoulder blades.
Sometimes
it was all I could do to keep my clothes on. To keep from moaning
aloud. Once a bucket—an occasional, embarrassing slosh over the top
if jostled—now a sieve, desire leaking from every pore. Which is why
I tried so hard to be harder. To use the world as my whetstone,
sharpening
myself against each day. My body cried out for armor. Big boned,
broad shouldered, I was built for it: forced into a dress with shoulder
pads,
I was the 90s' littlest linebacker. So I began to run, clanking
like a tank around cul-de-sacs. Began to climb, building biceps
strong enough to stiff-arm the world away. Even my heart grew

heavy, grew into one more thing to carry.

Introduction to Love
Emily R. Jones

Are scattered brain cells the sign of love?
And irrational thought formation the indicator of adoration?
Her voice made me inept
Unable to remain standing
Always falling
Stumbling
The entirety a complete degradation
And yet my heart has never felt more complete
Bursting with adorned happiness

White noise

Isabel J. Wallace

I fell in love when she heard music in white noise:
syncopated, vast, and terrible in the way
every angel has been since I met her.
This love is only discernible by the space between us two,
by absence and distance and other things that don't sound romantic anymore.
I've lost my taste for sacrifice.
I want to hear music and to be afraid,
to know I have something to lose because the space beside me is occupied.
I want to find her, to know her, to walk with her.
I want to feel solidity and to see who we could be.
The future is a beast with broken teeth, and our skin is thinning with age.
And oh, apprehension— waiting for it to take a bite out of us
I'd twist its neck into something new, for her.
I want to build something new with her.
I love her like someone comprehending the size of the universe
(for the first time, awed)
vast and terrifying and wonderful.
She heard music where there was none,
and I loved her even after my last chord was quiet

A Girl and her Fairytale
A. Staley

A little girl plays with dolls
She's a girl…
Dolls are expected

The dolls create a fairytale
A fairytale of…
Never ending love

That fairytale follows us as we grow
We kiss…We lust…We fall
We're shattered at the deepest level
We try and try
Only to fail time and again

Then we fall…
Everyday… over and over
We've found a love
That makes fairytales look weak
This love… takes our breath
It shatters us in the most beautiful way

Sapphos
Grace Desmarais

Sea Shanty: Drunken Sailor

Sean Heather K. McGraw

"What shall we do with a drunken sailor?
What shall we do with a drunken sailor?
What shall we do with a drunken sailor?
Early in the morning."

"Way, hey and up she rises, way, hey and up she rises
Way, hey and up she rises, ear-lye in the morning."
I put her in the shower as she's my lover,
Wild night we had, just to recover.
"Way, hey and up she rises, ear-lye in the morning"

"Way, hey and up she rises, way, hey and up she rises"
Way, hey and up she rises, ear-lye in the morning."
I was sleeping with the Captain's daughter,
I was sleeping with the Captain's daughter,
I was sleeping with the Captain's daughter,
"Early in the morning."

"Way, hey and up she rises, way, hey and up she rises"
Way, hey and up she rises, ear-lye in the morning."
Get up, eat and pour coffee all over,
Get up, eat and pour coffee all over,
Get up, ear and pour coffee all over,
"Early in the morning."

"Way, hey and up she rises, way, hey and up she rises"
Way, hey and up she rises, ear-lye in the morning."
She had a husband whose name was Tim,
She had a husband whose name was Tim,
She had a husband whose name was Tim,
"Early in the morning."

"Way, hey and up she rises, way, hey and up she rises"
Way, hey and up she rises, ear-lye in the morning."

This Is What Loves Looks Like

She's ever so glad that she left him
She's ever so glad that she left him
She's ever so glad that she left him
"Early in the morning."

"Way, hey and up she rises, way, hey and up she rises"
Way, hey and up she rises, ear-lye in the morning."
A woman's heart is all she wants now
A woman's heart is all she wants now
A woman's heart is all she wants now
"Early in the morning."

"Way, hey and up she rises, way, hey and up she rises"
Way, hey and up she rises, ear-lye in the morning."
I'm her special woman sailor
I'm her special woman sailor
I'm her special woman sailor
"Early in the morning."

"Way, hey and up she rises, way, hey and up she rises"
Way, hey and up she rises, ear-lye in the morning."
She likes her butch Officer to save her
She likes her butch Officer to save her
She likes her butch Officer to save her
"Early in the morning."

"Way, hey and up she rises, way, hey and up she rises"
Way, hey and up she rises, ear-lye in the morning."
Come back home and we'll start all over
Come back home and we'll start all over
Come back home and we'll start all over
"Early in the morning."

"Way, hey and up she rises, way, hey and up she rises"
Way, hey and up she rises, ear-lye in the morning."
Come back home and we'll start all over
Come back home and we'll start all over

Come back home and we'll start all over
"Early in the morning."

"Way, hey and up she rises, way, hey and up she rises"
Way, hey and up she rises, ear-lye in the morning."
Living with you is such a spark now
Living with you is such a spark now
Living with you is such a spark now
"Early in the morning."

A green marbled malachite egg

Carla Toney

Amber, onyx, amethyst
are displayed in the window,
a lapis lazuli lion and rose
quartz elephant locked
safely behind glass inside.
On the counter in a wicker basket
is a clutch of green marbled
malachite eggs, like those
of an ancient reptilian bird
still waiting, after centuries,
to hatch.

I've already bought you reproductions
of Albinus's copperplate engravings:
skeletons, flayed of flesh and skin,
waltz with cherubim. I've bought you
a golden roofed pagoda, painted
on a Chinese lacquer try, but
what kind of love would we hatch
if I bought you a green marbled
malachite egg?

Crossing Borders

For Nikola

Maranda Greenwood

I have a hard time admitting when the distance
makes me feel insecure and I say or do the wrong thing.

the shape of your eyebrows go flat,
your head turns to the side like

you want to look away from something painful.
My shortcomings make me feel ashamed,

A poorly timed joke, a delayed response
the unintentional public pull away causes me to cringe

in regret, my toes curl in my shoes and my palms go hot
and my engagement ring feels cold, there is an actual ache beneath

my sternum that can't be soothed. It makes me
want to cry into your chest and feel your arms tighten

around me but instead I suggest, a break.
My fearful defense, and as soon as I say this out loud

and you reluctantly say okay—I panic that you and me
will never be you and me— and then I can't leave my bed.

I think of your small hands wrapped around my arms,
how my heart pounds over your lips pressed against my palm.

I have found I can't stand to be touched by anyone but you
and how stupid it is that I resist you only because I'm afraid

of the moments like this: where I'm alone
in the house and you are everywhere but here,

This Is What Loves Looks Like

the silence between your mouth and my ear
will cause me to listen so hard that I disintegrate into

nothing more than this pile of jumbled words.
My phone won't vibrate me back into a whole person

because I told you not to call.

I am afraid that I will fail you, that your eyebrows will go flat too often
That I won't be able to explain why I still fear you,

that you won't always like me and then you won't love me
and I will have met the only woman who can hold me how you do.

The weight of my losses cripples me at night and you clutch me to your chest
like I am weightless and you could carry me indefinitely.

I am afraid that I will lose all of this and you'll be gone
over something that just made me feel insecure.

I think of that time in Southern Tasmania how we kissed in the dark
next to the ocean while the plankton glowed, and how I know that your

electricity is the only thing that moves my blood, the spark
feels faint when we are apart, a small firefly travelling across the ocean.

I believe you are the blue rain rings in the bioluminescence,
you spread through my cells like this and I worry

when I try to keep it, that I won't capture it and it fades away,
the only thing left with your faint glow will be the stone in my ring.

This is what happens in my brain when we fight.

SMITTEN

Just so you know, I am sorry I suggest silence, never agree to this.

Instead, tell me that even when I'm wrong and we feel the weight of long distance,
that there's only one more border to cross before you're my wife,

and that you think about every time we find each other on the other side
of borders and how our hands lace together like an upside-down prayer

and we keep going.

There was a Time
Tia M. Hudson

"*I cannot go on with us.*"
I'd like to say it's because you are wrong.
But me, I'm not right either.
Like a wind that starts
by rustling the very tops of trees;
and ends by bowing the supple ones
to the ground
and uprooting the obstinate, proud
and well rooted,
I cannot explain where it came from
or why it grew so strong
but we both are exhausted
from the bending and buttressing
against its force.
Now there are limbs and boughs
in the road
scattered there between us
we still lean toward each other
without touching.
There is only a dull green and brown
of broken branches
a flat grey of dim light above
and black tarmac below.
There was a time, once,
before the wind blew
and the ground shifted.
Once.
I remember that time.

Letters
Maranda Greenwood

I think of us quiet on the tailgate
of an old truck, legs swinging,
drive-in screen image not yet in focus,
the dusty old place almost empty.
I've tried to tell you, you feel familiar
a hundred times, but just stare at my feet
and offer to pop the top off your beer.

I think about the 9 unsent letters
in my desk drawer where I couldn't
get the order of the words right.
I want to tell you that I don't want
anything from you, just your company,
just your mind, but instead
what makes it into the letter—

your blue eyes and your big jewelry, your long nails and that you wear clothes that are too old for you— that I believe the weight of your bag has changed the anatomy of your shoulder, one side dropped three inches lower—that your shoes are not sensible for any adventure with me, and that your eyebrows are too thin— but I find it all very charming, and wish you would change nothing. Towards the end of the letter, I admit that the sudden idea of kissing you only intruded once when you wore lipstick, and how I almost asked you to wipe it off right there in the middle of the carnival. It's very cliché, I picture us over and over at different locations, just quiet, like little shaking magnets that only threaten collision if they face each other.

Two Bitches (Cabin Poem)

Michelle Paige

We were topless in a wooden hut
Miles away from towns and streets with names
Standing skin on skin with mouths apart
Kisses stained and tart from too much wine
While the woods outside were dark and still
Faces lit with fire's dancing glow
Thrilled and eager hands with flesh were filled
Urgent movements careful like a doe
All the world around us fell away
Bit by bit I felt it disappear
Only you and I were what remained
Sticky sweet with marshmallows to share
Eat you like a complicated smore
Leave me with an appetite for more

A Simple Wedding Song

Emily Alice DeCicco

Salut d'amour has been
a thunderous composition.

Repetitive, blaring violin
making conversations
impossible to follow.
I am bending
to the will of a
crescendoing piano.

Lost in the throes
of how you took me
and filled what I believed
could never be anything
but hollow.

The chlorine on your skin ... summer 2018

Nadia G.

The chlorine on your skin tastes like Summer 2018
you've gone miles around the world on one street of Chicago
it'll come if you want it, but you never seem to want to
take direction from tides and the path of least resistance
did my bum hip remind you of what it feels like to be resisted?
there's no adventure to you, just more of the same
I'm tired of walking, do I still remind you of the rain?
I tried to put away the memory, that smell of your skin,
it's older than even you and you can't own it again

in the aether, all the signs
Lindz McLeod

This is escapism.
(You go to a different country)
You know you can outpace your problems, at least for a while.
You go home with a familiar stranger.
This isn't what you would normally do.
You're surprised by how pleasant it was-
you think about this and decide that
this isn't the right word, not even close
this is too old-fashioned, too clunky, too cliched
for such a delicate...
you can do better than that.
Try harder.
(You weave your words together to hold it tighter than a memory)
But nothing else comes to mind
because when she smiles it pulls upwards in your gut,
like a blinking cursor,
hovering above your blankest page.
You picture how it looked when the rain started
to drop kisses into her hair.
You fly out on a Thursday, late,
so goddamn late that every blink hurts,
and there are plenty open-and-shuts.
(You spend a cumulative total of
thirty thousand years
on that flight, thinking about her)
You assume you'll never see her again.
You can't remember by which standard you judge
anything anymore,
but you wonder if maybe this hurts more
than it should.

Trying to Hide an Ocean
Carrie Groebner

I study your voice with hunger-
As for now it is all I have.

Memorizing cadences
I Listen for the eloquence of your phrasing with careful attention.
Read to me I say-
as I want to taste every word of your voice.
Wanting to memorize and imprint my soul with the desire for you behind every
tone,
inflection,
pause-
the finality of a phrase that seals our love for one another-
I want you in words as, again- it is all I have.

"Let me read to you the lyrics of the great Mexican Composer Augustin Lara" you say

You sigh…
You know I am deeply listening to every word you speak
Wanting you more with every offering.
My desire like outstretched arms of Benediction.
You know you have me for all Eternity and in this moment, this very moment-
As no one will ever match the depth of your presence.
I want to love you the way Augustin Lara Loved Maria Felix-
She haunted him
Every woman after her would pale in comparison.
No one could ever hold his heart like Maria.

You begin to read the lyrics of Augustin Lara's song: Mujer Divina:

"Mujer, Mujer, divina
Tienes el veneno que fascina

SMITTEN

En tu mirar
Mujer alabastrina
Eres Vibracion de sontatina passional…"

Tears Streaming down my face as I listen to your voice;
I am begging all the ascended masters, high priestesses,
Archangels…, all of Heaven
Let me keep her. Please let me keep her…
Let me hold on to her, this Astoundingly Beautiful Woman who owns my heart.

It is all I will ever ask of love.

As she reaches the last word of the poem:
"Eres la Razon de mi existir, mujer…"

There is silence,
the way it feels after great prayer-
And I say to her:" If you, your essence could be one of the great poems of our time,
What would you title it?"
And you say with clarity and quiet exaltation:
"Trying to Hide an Ocean."

*Lyrics of song: *Mujer Divina* by composer Augustin Lara

Love Poem: Colors V

after Donika Kelly

Talia Rizzo

Has your body been made   into a canvas by the woman
you love? She sits between   your legs   naked, her thin
figure straddling. Her face   red at the site of your bare body.
A plate in hands, stale paint   on a cheap brush. You feel your
stomach in dark green. A set   of castles   redwood trees
around a bellybutton sun. The cold   thick of the paint sending a
shiver   down your back.   Goosebumps   as tiny green
hills as connectable constellations   as the animators of a blackberry.
Thighs molted into dense   strokes of dark blue. Bristles
crumbling into the medium,   scratching against the skin.
Nipples clad with crusting   yellow paint. Each streak
running a line   a part of   you. Purple down your ribs.
Orange under your armpits.   Burgundy in swirls on your
neck. Turquoise navel, a race up   the spinal cord. Magenta heart.
Here you are, nails through   your veins, hung above your
bed frame   staining your   walls with the color of yourself.

Thoughts in the Shower

after Philip Schaefer

Talia Rizzo

What do people talk about after sex? I fall asleep
with the lights on. Being in love means
sacrificing the better towel. The long striped
purple one with heavy threading. Falling out
of love comes with little warning. My mother says
if someday I witness a crime, I won't be able
to pick out the subject in a line-up. I don't look
up when I walk. Or in elevators. What is it like
to have a basement? As a child, I crawled up to
the attic for our summer couch cushions, the
splintered nails nicking my thin skin. My
blood the color of plums, tattooing the wood
floor in thin brushless burgundy streaks. At night,
I murmur answers into my lover's hair. She forgets
the question. We wake up with our spinal cords
intertwined ants walking trails from one piece of
flesh to another. I am trying to build a colony. The
grasshoppers keep coming, their toothpick legs
taking taking taking. Everything raked clean
except for the queen. This winter, I have been left
to eat the skeleton of leaves. Aspens are the sweetest.
I am given dirt to swallow until my mouth becomes a
feeder box. My teeth are the seeds. Birds flock to me.
Animal bones equal mortality. I pretend I am not scared.
I pretend to feel pleasure. Weed doesn't taste like
fruit it tastes like stale bark. I like making love with
a tree in my throat. Red wine as the soil. I am the roots.
Her body is the course. I crack rocks open and bury our
names in their granite. I sometimes cook sometimes cheat
sometimes can't meet my eyes while brushing my teeth.
I know I am guilty. I know my neighbors are doing heroin
at dawn because their bathroom light is still on the tape
pulled back from cellophane crevices. We use the same shampoo

in a   green bottle. If the vote for me   on my knees   a ring
in my pant pocket   was tomorrow,   my father would walk
to the ballot from his office and vote *for*. I understand this
as a form of progress. Tomorrow,
I will say   thank you

the crux of my old problem

Rachel M. McGayhey

the subtlety of your familiar hands
the pale grace and fine bones of your wrist
the neutral middle distance in your eyes
the firelight still crackling in mine

it dawns on me:
i should have seen this coming

the icy shock, my deepest self laid bare
felled, flailing, strings cut and you aloof
flayed by the lack of color in your eyes
more vivid than the distance now between us

the crux of my old problem, still unchanged
i am not like any other girl
well— neither, it seems, are you
i see your face everywhere, still,
i seek your face everywhere
i cede my fate

there at the cradle of two great rivers oasis at the desert's secret heart
all the puzzles i had laid for you
clues and crumbs to find your way to me and you, like Ariadne, sought me out

the lengths of yarn that marked your way to me
tangle now around me, coiling, cold
chafing raw and sticky red as iron shackles
dragging me heavy down with every step

stubbornly i grasp them, even as i sink
my last clinging link to you, my golden cloud,
my last hope of finding my way out

Andy & KP
Katherine DeGilio

Smoke rings cascade between fairy laughs
while limerence bumbles through apiary paths
the buzzing concords and crescendos with smiles
willing to fly eternity's miles
fingertips brush poppies and leaves
never tired of the day to day reprise
where stars don't collide, but clasp hands
the red string of destiny wrapped tight in bands
and sun and moon beams do so conspire
they compromise

Getting Groceries
Aviva Lilith

waiting for
 walls to cave in.

white, white walls
 covered in this-and-thats,
smothered with love: secret love.
 it is suffocating to breathe
tight air when ceilings threaten to fall, at
 once it becomes an entire house, collapsing like a gray heart.

paint started chipping last night.
 we sat in bed, string pulling us opposite ways.
by now we are good at resisting.
 "should we hide all my stuff just in case?"
i say, turning silence inside out.
 "no, he won't come up i'm sure",
though the cold gray from the walls exhale into her eyes.
 we settle in, cactus sheets, no pillows.
art on the walls stare through us, eyes and eyes and eyes.
 salt lamp turns from pink to green
to blue to light blue to purple to red-and stays on red
 a bit too long.

 the shattered morning wakes her at 8:32 am.
alarm doesn't dare wake up until 11.
 sun seems lost today,
it does not contradict shadows, and everything seems rust.
 each particle, a disciple of the night.
air becomings a waterfall of lust, of rot, of sin-
 each hungry for warmth.
we are all hungry for warmth.
i try to understand these things.
 hiding kaleidoscopes my mind
into fragments.

This Is What Loves Looks Like

like leaves in a pool,
i try to filter them out.

we make our cheap coffee,
i trace lines of my mug,
they point dully, unenthused
but also ready to prick, prod, pray for my sins.
cactus mug for me,
bee mug for her.
some things sting when
threatened.

“come sit, drink coffee with me”
she paces
my voice echoes through the light.
she comes, takes sip,
but does not sit.
the window pulls her back,
as if the sky were raining answers,
or maybe obstinance instead.
either is worth getting buckets for.

ring,
ring.
“hello? i’ll be right down”,
she hangs up the phone.
her face white with capitulation.
standing up, i expect what is coming.
“he’s coming up”.
our eyes hold back the gray,
we should have done this last night.

scribble like lines to room,
throw my blankets under bed,
toss stuffed dog under also.
salt lamps calm anxiety,
hide it in a corner.

SMITTEN

my backpack,
eye drops,
headphones,
a drawing of me on wall
goes to closet where they so naturally belong.

everything else i try to grab within the minute
i gather, i hide
in the communal kitchen,
along with myself.
i crouch myself up
the way my blanket is,
and fit myself in a corner.
cornered by things that sting.
tears run down the way fire runs up,
burns burns burns,
acid pool full of leaves,
i swim through the salt
squinting my eyes
so no one can see how it hurts.

a minute goes by,
each second is a mile's walk down a highway
with a speed minimum of fifty,
miles away i sit,
dizzied by
nauseating thoughts:
i left my phone out.
just out on the bed.
how could i?
my shoes still sit in a box
in the room
and my deodorant too.
my tarot cards,
and all of my rocks.
i guess he wouldn't know
whose rocks are whose,

This Is What Loves Looks Like

right?

right?

just tell me i am right.

i hold my coffee mug
like it's the last thing that could save me,
i pray to it.
don't sting

she walks through the door,
it's over.
"you okay?"
i stand up, hug her.

that's all i have gathered on the
encounter with her father that day he came
to drop off groceries.

i will tell you about after
that:
as she has told me,
he recognized my tarot cards
as not being her's.
fathers are not observant,
luckily.
because i had also left my
oil diffuser,
books,
underwear on the floor
and my hair brushes.
i have two.

my heart didn't break while the
hiding went on,
nor did it break when i realized
i'll never be
accepted by her parents.

nor did it break when she cried
on my shoulder, because walls
were now squeezing us, lung to lung.
walls started flaking
because the world is so hateful, and
she doesn't even have parents
to tell her it's okay.
we were knee deep in paint chips now,

my heart broke
when i was putting things away.
i saw a photobooth photo of us,
just being friends
for a moment.
it was hidden,
along with
everything else.

Community

Izabell Jöraas Skoogh

We caught each other's eyes for a
millisecond.
She was dancing her most ridiculous dance
And I was letting everything go as well.
Then she leans over and screams through the music
- I have work in the morning
I smiled and replied,
Well, I have school
She asked me what I was studying
And our conversation ended with her saying
That she wouldn't have been able to do all the work she's doing
without her wife.
-wife-
On the spot
My heart was beating faster
The words were so encouraging
She ended the conversation with
"No matter how hard it gets. Keep going, keep fighting, it's worth it"
And
There
I
Stood
Just embracing all the love
I thought would never be a possibility for me.

Unforgettable
Wil Staley

I remember my first kiss…
my first real kiss from a girl;
the softness of her lips, the way it felt so wrong yet so right.
It was like sending a shockwave up my spine
I collapsed into that moment, felt every bit of it, fighting
what society told me was right and wrong.
That kiss was a taste of freedom.
I think it was the first time I had ever felt anything but pain
and beauty bloomed in my gut…
spoken with life at the tip of my tongue.
I had finally felt…me.

Chosen
Wil Staley

Love is…kisses so deep,
mosquito bites and soaked feet,
giggles in the dark, and never ceasing love notes.
It is looking into the eyes of the other person, knowing you were made for her
and you are better with her than you have been, or ever could be without.
Love is not needing her, but wanting her more than
you've ever wanted anything before.
It's as if your spirit was made to connect with hers…
your head meant for her shoulder… your heart for her hands;
and if given the chance,
you'd choose her all over again.

Sonnets to the love of my life

Susan M. Conway

-Our love is a map, and all roads lead straight to our comfy pants, wine, and practical magic for the umpteenth time.

-You have seeped into me, and now, I bleed you.

-I have been touched by your love, and it has made me a gorgeous misty morning.

-The grand finale might not be all fucking and fumbling like I thought, for most of my life. Perhaps, it is a tighter grasp on love, and a loosening grip on trauma. Thank you, for loving me so well.

-Fuck everyone, that ever made you doubt yourself; fuck everyone, that made you feel less than the epitome of love and redemption that you are to me.

-I take your skinned knees and raise them to my lips, kissing each and every wound. Some come to restore my love, and we have found redemption in one another. Thank you, thank you, thank you, for loving me so well.

Morning Senses
Cristina DeSouza

I write your tact on my bare skin.
I paint your smell in green on
the blank pages of a notebook
I forgot I had.

Licking the taste of your mouth
and keeping its texture on my lips
remind me of the flavor of dark
hot chocolate on a cold evening.

And what I hear is the sound of your
silence after love is made, while
I see your clear eyes staring at
the ceiling as if there were stars

shining there. The sense of your
presence by me is my sixth sense,
the one that radiates light and
warmth to my body that vibrates

softly when your fingers rub
gently against my breasts. And in the
wake of the day, we stay like this:
intertwined.
So much, that I no longer know
which limb is mine, which hand
Is yours. Minutes pass and morning
dawns on us, while birds chirp outside

Yellow and Red, Secretly Married.

Aviva Lilith

you are the type of girl
who bites into orange peels.
you eat an orange the way
one normally
eats apples,
starting with its
outside membrane, then
you sink your teeth into
the meat,
is this what being
vegetarian means?
i eat membranes too.
i eat purple, red,
green, peach, pink,
but i can't say i am brave
enough to eat
the orange one.

"doesn't that hurt?"
i ask you every time,
but i know it doesn't.
it takes someone pith
enough to eat acid skin,
and what better girl would
that be than someone
red as you?

i don't credit you enough
for it.
for eating peels.
i don't talk enough
about how it must taste
to bite straight into
trouble.

i do not tell you on
a daily basis how i
admire the fire
you breathe, when
it comes to the
subject of me.
i do not thank you
enough, for the love
you give to things
that cause pain.

if i am yellow,
you are red.
you always stand in front
of me, protecting me
from flames of
stinging people who say
“you’re sinning, by the way”
you protect me from
cold colors, whose intentions
i can’t see.
you protect me from the
orange peels,
by eating them
or me.

Neighbors of the Heart
Hallelujah R. Huston

I forget
how far away from
you I am
that I live in Florida
and you in Texas
I feel as if I am
just next door
watching you
on Wednesdays
haul the trash cans in
and tilt them up against
the stony wall
in their wooden frame
so neatly side by side
I wave from the other
manicured lawn
as if a pencil
in my mouth
clamped by my teeth
kept me from saying
hello
This is how near
you feel to me.

In The Closet

Jamie L. Smith

I spent summers with my legs tangled
with Alice's, to fit within our one cubic
meter of space. We smoked Sour Drops
until paint peeled from the yellowing walls.

Her father never knew his little angel spent
Monday through Friday blowing halos
against the door we carved our names into.
Vertigo spun us into a tight knot of limbs

on the dust-bunnied hardwood. As haze
drove her grandmother's mothball scent
from our nostrils, we nested in old flannel
nightgowns pulled from shelf to floor.

Coat hangers clinked, meet-hooks clanked
together, hungry for flesh. Paranoid, yes,
but we knew her mother was coming home.
We'd scuttle out, come later to collect

the roaches. We hauled ass to her bathroom.
Alice spewed. I sprayed perfume and body mist.
Her mom caught us showering off the hotbox
sweat that day. For fuck's sake girls,

you're too old for that. This isn't a locker room.
She never said so, but Alice's mom must have known
the scent we left behind couldn't have come
from burning our hair on her straightening iron.

There are four things ...

Erin Van Vuren

There are four things in
this life that will change
you. Love, music, art,
and loss. The first three
will keep you wild and
full of passion.
May you allow the last
to make you brave.

- Erin Van Vuren

@papercrumbs

The Girl Who Always Cries

Crystal Kinistino

Perched in darkness the owl can be heard to cry;
there are no worlds great enough
to contain the immeasurable anguish
issuing forth from that invisible soul

I peer towards the canopy of black sky–
starry, crimson, infinitely incomparable,
hoping to catch sight of she
who always cries but never can be seen

I sense her watching me,
her sharp gaze shining in clairvoyance,
her foreboding wings opening and closing–
as they cleave towards the quartz center,
where these parallel fates hold us tethered

All the world hangs from that tree,
and the moon in bewilderment also,
an enchanting tapestry,
whose binding synchronicity
is the conduit for our pain

The earth prepares herself
as if in nocturnal wait —
her mouth a clotted wasteland,
her hair a metallic river of blood
in which the muses drown

Heeding her perpetual cry
the tongue is paralyzed,
succumbed to muteness,
there is no language profuse enough
to convey her bruising music
this is what I am made up of;

SMITTEN

this dark matter reaching into eternity,
this pitch of perennial sadness
bitten through the birch-bark
which is her birthmark

Of all the girls I will ever know,
her cry is the only one which will always
baffle me with its beauty,
because it was as though
I could feel her sorrow chiming
in the cathedral of my veins,
winding its hymns through my blood,
never knowing precisely from where it precipitated

Was my cry her voice or was her voice my crying,
and why did other girls believe they could compete
against such an occultic force, such a mythical bird as that?

I will never catch sight of her, it is impossible-
she nestles behind my eyes,
she chants through my temples
in the synapses of a charred gloom,
no divining stick, no mirror will draw her out.

Patterns of Love

Anonymous

Revisiting Tohono Chul, For Alice, 13 Years Later

Jamie L. Smith

Rabbits still run the courtyard wild and cacti spears
sharp-fence the park perimeter with palm-sized purple blooms

crowning their heads and a hummingbird tongues pollen
from seeds, emerald cheek gold-dusted as he lifts

above the square—hovers—an apostrophe hung above gardens
above mazed paths empty of people now, dusk clouds

edging in. And what is an apostrophe but a sign
of possession, and whatever possessed us to dance

in that desert downpour all those years ago? Alice,
the girl I hungered for like saguaros crave rain, you

raised me into the breeze and we fell shrieking into mud.
What is memory if not the rain-drenched

mud-slathered you existing within me? Your wet form
folded into my labyrinth—suspended—so I feel your grit

tangled hair and cold sand studding your soaked shirt.
Standing below this low-slung sky, I can almost forget

I don't know you now. Violet-mouthed flowers pray down
a grayscaled paradise. The first drop falls centimeters

from my eye, a translucent globe splashed open on red stairs
where tomorrow descends a girl in a pink dress, maybe

new patent leather shoes squeaking slightly with each step,
another entry into the bright kaleidoscope of days without you.

Love Her

Char Trolinder

It's said that love is beautiful and brave. Perhaps being a woman that loves women is nothing short of extraordinarily heroic and gorgeously bold. A path so few know intimately, and so many lack understanding. It can be lonely and isolating, but to burn with the desire a woman has for another woman can be majestic and world shaking. Love her unapologetically because the world needs to quake under the feet of that kind of love.

New York Love Poem

Liz DeGregorio

I bragged to a friend
that I was easily able to convince women they were
seducing me in front of the Lincoln Center Fountain.
Little old me, looking up through
        uncharacteristically mascaraed eyes
When did I finally realize they were telling their friends
        the same story?

The Usual

Liz DeGregorio

I was on the floor (the usual story), you were on the phone (the usual call). I asked if you ever wanted to bleach your brain, remove all the "bad" parts, the parts that had leached deep into your memory, the parts that eroded your trust, and caused you to call your girlfriend from the bathroom floor (yes, that should've been specified before, it's true).

Kanoodling [in the forest Like A pair of Heartless lesbians]

Janis Sommers

This is a found poem. A found poem is one written from words found in another place. All words other than the found phrase are mine.

Kanoodling in the forest
Like
A pair of
Heartless lesbians

I saw you
With him
On the bed
You
Slept in
With him

I saw your children
On the bed
With him
With you
Laughing

My heart lurched
My heart ached
My heart longed
To be there, too
With you

No
Not

This Is What Loves Looks Like

This cannot
continue

I stole you from him
Who you
Thought you'd be safe with,
Sowing life as a family

No
Not
Cannot continue
He
Could not
Concede
To me
Nor I
Could not
Conceive
Our road

Kanoodling
in the forest
like
a pair
of
heartless
Lesbians

We scramble
Down
Into
The
mountain
clove
Champagne swaddled
In a towel
In my Adirondack

SMITTEN

Backpack
Silver glasses
Trimmed
In
Gold

Exploring
Questioning
Touching
Kissing
Surprise
Confusion
Laughing
With
You
Wild
Tension building
My heart
Racing
Electric fingers touching
I don't know
What
I am doing

Who
knew
there
were
so many paths
Before us
You
Me

Kanoodling
In
The
Forest

This Is What Loves Looks Like

Like a
Pair of
Heartless Lesbians

He
Who
Rejected you
When he saw us
You
Who left
Your family split

You
Who could not
Continue
With him
Could not
Continue
With
Me
You
Did not
Show up
To dance
Under
Disco lights

You chose
I did not
I lost you
I grieved
I denied
I was
OK

You

SMITTEN

I don't know what you did
or
Did not deny

I,
Who
You thought
You were
Safe with,
You
The Mother

Who
Knew
Lavender trail before us.

self portrait as rain

Kai Coggin

opposite
of barren
I am nothing but soak
nothing but drip
and drench
and downpour now

perhaps I have
already
fallen
and risen again
precipitated fate

these cycles
of drowning into oceans
defend my tendency
to follow things
all the way down
to where you are
a willing drop of water
waiting to merge

perhaps this is the only way
I will ever truly
touch your skin
drip down your cheek
trace your lips
o' drink me in

I wait for the clouds to release me
from this crystallized linger

I converge
with a system of heat and updrafts

SMITTEN

become unstable patterns of turbulence
so I can weather this want
break
open
deluge
the space
in you
waiting
to be filled
with me
I gather in puddles
pool
at your collarbones
the small of your back
the crease of your smile

become a sea
in your open palms

Her

Kai Coggin

I might've been ten
when I realized
the magnets inside me were
spinning toward her
whoever *her* was
she
was my everything
my longing to be close
my ache to be seen
my dream to be kissed by
touched by
missed by
her
whoever *her* was
she
was my love
and I could not help
but be enamored

the feelings
did not die down
they grew into silent flowers in my chest
until a meadow sprung from my mouth when I spoke
until petals only saying
she loves me
spilled from my lips and became my words at
that age
I did not have the word *gay* did
not have the word *lesbian* the
word *queer* just this fear
to explain my frame of reference
around my undeniable attraction to
her.

SMITTEN

There was always a *her* through
the years of my youth a too-far
face
I could fix my eyes and heart upon
like a star guiding me out of my blackhole secret
never close enough to touch
never close enough to whisper
never close enough to be real in my arms
I was taught those fires would burn me forever
and sin was named after a woman
but
I wanted her skin
on my mouth
so much.

The first time I kissed a girl at 17
I might have been a fault line the way I trembled
the way the earth moved all around our fresh young bodies
I remember her wild curls
falling across my face
the way she laughed the taste of her yes the
ceiling fan
spinning rings over our heads
and I may have never returned to earth that day
the way she sent me hovering into the atmosphere with
only the fear that this moment might not be real
and these kisses and her cheek and her neck and her shoulder
and her
and her
and her
moving up so close
to the wild magnet of me might
just be a fleeting dream but it
wasn't a dream
it was

love

real love
my first love
and her name stays with me
folded into my skin
and I can remember her in poems
and be right there again
two budding young flowers
opening to each other's fingers
how the memories linger after 20 years she
is married now
to a man
has two beautiful children
we don't speak
and I like
to think
it is because
there is still a part of her
that remembers
how I trembled
and to no fault of hers
or mine
love sometimes
makes strangers out of lovers but
can I write her into a poem and
thank her
always for
being real.

Snow Carpets
Susan M. Conway

You know how you get that tingly, buzzing urge to run screaming into the spotless, perfectly laid carpet of fallen snow?

You're kinda like, HOLY SHIT, you're perfect! I kinda need to rub my body all over you, like a dog scratching an itch to leg jerking perfection.

That's what it feels like to watch you sleep, filtered rays of sunlight dancing across your face and over your platinum blonde hair. I'm kinda like, HOLY SHIT, you're perfect!

I mean to say, you are perfectly laid.
I mean to say, I wanna run to you.
I mean to say baby, I wanna mess you up, rub my body all over you, like a dog scratching an itch to leg jerking perfection.

I wanna make snow angels in your shadowy parts.

I wanna etch my name in all of the places that melt from my heavy breathing just so I get to keep showing up, tracing each curve carefully, over and over again in the winters of our unruly love.

I wanna keep coming back to you, missing your sharp bite when I am not near, and the way I turn red when I touch you, for the rest of my life.

Give you a wildfire

Erin Van Vuren

You will ask
for a match,
and I will
give you
a wildfire.
I don't know
how to love
small.

- Erin
Van Vuren
@papercrumbs

Summer Crushes
Kirsten Fedorowicz

She asks me about the boy I'm seeing,
and his name suddenly becomes unimportant.
James, Jake, or Jason,
an ordinary boy with his perfectly sculpted calves,
big nose, temporary adoration of me,
suddenly slips from my mind
as she pulls off her shirt.
With grace and rhythm,
she uncovers her toned and tanned body
in its black bikini,
ready to swim in the river below.
She dives in first, fearless, and I follow,
The water rushing around me,
holding me in its familiar grip.
I become a leaf caught in the current,
Buoyant with realization while simultaneously sinking,
turning somersaults in a river
that only wants me to go one way.
When we break the spell of the water,
We perch on a nearby log,
sunning ourselves like turtles, soft underbellies turned in.
I manage to forgive her for not liking Jane Austen,
she does not judge me for the way I think
the red cap is the best part of
The Catcher in the Rye.
Once dry, we change on the sandy banks of the shore,
Her slipping clothes undergarments in that
Specific sports girl way,
Wiggling a bikini out from under a sports bra,
She attributes her abilities to softball, vocally,
tells me about locker rooms, other women.
The only thing odd about this is that she has pointed it out,
The way women get dressed and undressed together,
an unspoken law of comfort,

punctuated only by playful teases of *nice ass*,
by the comparison of breasts.
And I wonder if, one day, a curiosity was sparked at the sight
of a smooth back.
If, like me, kept it locked in her heart,
A secret to take out and polish on occasion.
I examine her words,
as if I would ever find the key
to an alternate universe of *we*,
A key to a door I will never unlock.

Morning Chores
Rachael Ikins

I know I should
dress. 10:20 a.m. still
wearing a paint-spattered
disintegrating sweatshirt
gown and battered Birkenstocks.
Laundry loads between
changes, dryer-hum, coffee
maker half undone, private
parts strewn across the counter
like so much embarrassed underwear.
Sweeping, dog-walks.
I need to feed our pig. But,
the lilacs.
The lilacs! Ancient bushes
roped together by some lover's
long-gone hand, spew heart's-blood,
froth over the backyard hill and lace-
white. I clamber wet to slippery knees.

Tall grass paints my thighs. Cold.
Rain-speckled apple petals fool
me for snow. I bury frozen fingers,
my face in public purple flower
mounds. Curl around my cheeks and
silky leaves labial against my breath-caught
mouth.

High in the old dying maple
a hairy woodpecker trills into
her feathers about her lover. Satisfied,
oh, yes! I could lay me down, bare-skinned blue,
right here and now
between these mighty mother
lilac thighs.

Pulse
Melissa Fadul

The surgeon stood in a brook of blood—some stream that seemed to be emptying itself into the mouth of a lake in the west wing of the emergency room hallway. Its bright white walls shined louder than the fluorescent lights that stood in total existential contrast to the crimson puddle spreading like lava unconfined. The blood wasn't one person's, but more than fifty whose dancing venture the night of June 12th 2016, suddenly halted—A young man walked into *Pulse*, a gay nightclub in *Orlando, Florida* and soaked the crowd in bullets bolted from a semi-automatic rifle and pistol. Senior resident doctor, Joshua Corsa, on duty that night at *Orlando Regional Medical Center* was introduced to anonymous victims' blood before their mouths could produce names. His new sneakers soaked up so much of the liquid that by the end of his thirty-hour shift, the laces, fibers and threads bled.

Six days before and less than one thousand miles North of *Pulse*, my now wife, bent down on one knee under a tree in a downtown *Brooklyn Park*, and asked me to spend the rest of my life with her. Coincidentally, her ring was in my bag next to the poem I wrote for her proposal. Without a spec of ambivalence, we agreed that our love could only be matched by one another. Strangers took some pictures of us—They seemed happy to capture our hour—I couldn't tell you their sexual status or what bathroom they chose to use—I didn't know if any of them had an arrest record or ever spent time in jail. No one rejected us when we asked them to take part in one of the most significant moments of our lives. No one said anything or pointed when we kissed. We stayed a little longer. In the distance, liberty stood, bleeding of rust—behind ribbons of fog that enveloped her, haze and mist alluded to the allegory by foreshadowing something invisible—that even power—even autonomy in all its independence required protection sometimes.

One week later, we sat on our love seat—arms around each other while news crawlers sped across the television screen with little information about the *Pulse* shooter and his victims. After an hour, images began to repeat—The third time the station showed us the shot of the two bloodied men running and carrying their unconscious friend, I said to myself, *maybe he'll wake up this time.* It was juvenile and ridiculous to think—However, that day nothing seemed more insane than people jumping out windows in the back room of *Pulse* and hiding in bathroom stalls just to be able to wake up the next morning and wonder how to come out.

That could have been us, I said to my love. She responded, *yup*. On national television, a mother reported her son missing. She hoped he wasn't face down on a floor with dance still left in him. Who was he? Was he the type of guy to carry a condom in his wallet and a fortune from a cookie saying *about time I came out*? Would I ever know? How many bodies became evidence lined in chalk that resembled Cocaine? I kissed her forehead and squeezed her tighter while whispering, *that could have been us.*

My Heart Villanelle

Carol H. Jewell

You are my love, you are my heart
You soothe whatever bug I've caught
Two peas, one pod, right from the start.

I feel you even when we are apart
Love like ours cannot be bought
You are my love, you are my heart.

You make my Muse recall her Art
From your smile, your words, the flowers you brought
Two peas, one pod, right from the start.

Whether rock n roll or Amadeus Mozart,
I sing your song; your wishes--my thought
You are my love, you are my heart.

Two wives, each other's counterpart,
We bring to our marriage what the other sought
Two peas, one pod right from the start.

Friends don't know how we were from our start,
They look at us and say: haven't they ever fought?
You are my love, you are my heart,
Two peas, one pod right from the start.

I love you more than Mariska Hargitay

Carolyn Martin

And so the day begins with you
explicating last night's dream
about the way she stroked your cheek
with her arresting smile and lured
you toward a dark-eyed kiss before
you fought her off explaining
it would be criminal beyond
the ordered bounds of law
because the fact is I'm downstairs
in muddy garden clothes and sleepy hair
waiting for your lips so I can ditch
my coffee cup and stubborn poem
to wage my outdoor chores
and you're telling me you're telling her
you never swore a vow or wear
a wedding ring but when stray nights
tempt you toward a luscious offering
you walk away you're telling me
you are faithful even in your dreams.

Previously published in *The Wild Ones*.

Mementos
Christine E. Ray

I keep you in a basket
at the foot of my bed
that I can grab quickly
in case of fire
or other emergency
you are tucked in among
the postcards from exotic places
fading photographs
handwritten letters
greeting cards signed with love
and other mementos
of my past
that I can't bear to lose

Love is Our Theory
Sean Heather K. McGraw

Stonewall 1969
What was in that land before Time
Mattachine men
And Daughters of Bilitis
Homophile Movement in German spoken
British Well of Loneliness is Radclyffe's token.
Havelock Ellis and Krafft-Ebing disease and perversion,
Sassoon's poems and Freudian coercion.
Homo or hetero same or opposite
Desire is desire and always apposite.
Stonewall riot 1969 we refuse
To be burdened or to take abuse.
Gay Liberation Front and Gay Alliance
Lesbians singing to their affianced.
Baths and bars and leather jackets
Holly Near and Chris W. in album packets.
There are women shouting to be heard,
There are men not boys to be lured.
Black Salsa Sisters dance in rows,
Audre Lorde stepping on all our toes.
Adrienne Rich changes the world,
Jewelle Gomez lets Gilda's banner be unfurled.

GLSEN and GLAAD, NCLR and HRC,
Alphabet soup of our yearning to be free.
AIDS crisis brings tears to our eyes,
Death claims those whom we can't say our goodbyes.
Deaths from disease and deaths from murder
Shepard and Teena, Araujo and Lister
Violence against us burns that blister.
DeGeneres, Lang, Etheridge and Wright,
Frank, Kuehl, Milk, Rasmussen in our fight.
This is our theory of inclusivity-
civil rights for you and me.

This Is What Loves Looks Like

Coming out and breaking stone walls,
Teaching, singing and being in movie halls.
Love is our theory beyond all else,
Love brings out our better self.
Love is happy, love is gay,
loving everyone who comes our way.
Love is our theory that we belong,
Love is our sword and love is our song.

Author Bios

Avital Abraham hails from Fanwood, NJ, but is currently a sophomore at Ithaca College in Ithaca, NY studying Sociology with a double minor in Environmental Studies and the Ithaca College Honors program. Avital has been writing poetry and prose since second grade and now writes mostly spoken word poetry. She was a featured performer at the 2018 and 2019 annual Spit That! poetry showcase. When she isn't writing, Avital also enjoys collaging, crocheting, and gardening.

Didi Artier attended the Sorbonne Université - Faculté des lettres, and the Lycée Richelieu. Since then she has had her work published in *Dumas de Demain*. She currently makes her home in Paris, and is originally from Rueil-Malmaison, France. Didi writes in French and English and stands up for women's rights whenever possible.

Kindra M. Austin is an author, editor, and micro-publisher from Chesaning, Michigan, USA. To date, Austin has published three poetry books (*Constant Muses*, *TWELVE*, and *All the Beginnings of Everything*), a novel (*Magpie in August*), and one novella (*For You, Rowena*). She also contributed to and served as one of four editors for *We Will Not Be Silenced: The Lived Experience of Sexual Harassment and Sexual Assault Told Powerfully Through Poetry, Essay and Art.*

Kim D. Bailey is a 2016 Pushcart Nominee for nonfiction, and a 2018 Best of the Net Nominee for poetry. Currently, she works as a paid reviewer for Carpe Librum books, and does some freelance work. She is published in several online and print journals and in audio, including but not limited to *Firefly Magazine*, *Tuck Magazine*, *The Scarlet Leaf Review*, *Writer's Digest*, *Anti Heroine Chic*, *The Song Is*, *Indigent Press*, *The 52 Men Podcast*, and *Tupelo Press*. Kim was a columnist for *Five 2 One Literary Magazine* from June 2016 to October 2017, writing to *Breaking the Legacy of Silence*. She has also held editorial positions with *Firefly Magazine* and *Sick Lit Magazine*.

Sonia Beauchamp lives on the North Shore of Oahu. Her poems can be found in *Screen Door Review* and elsewhere. When she's not working as a massage therapist, you might find her surrounded by feral chickens or spinning fire in the moonlight. Find out more at soniakb.com.

Henri Bensussen's poems and stories have appeared in various journals, including *Eclipse*, *Blue Mesa Review*, *Sinister Wisdom,* and others, and in the anthologies, *Beyond the Yellow Wallpaper: New Tales of Madness,* and Lisa Locasio, ed., *Golden State 2017*. A chapbook of poems, *Earning Colors*, was published by Finishing Line Press in 2015. She has a B.A. in Biology.

Sarah Bigham lives in Maryland with her kind chemist wife, three independent cats, an unwieldy herb garden, several chronic pain conditions, and near-constant outrage at the general state of the world tempered with love for those doing their best to make a difference. A Pushcart and Best of the Net nominee, Sarah's poetry, fiction and nonfiction have appeared in a variety of great places for readers, writers and listeners. Find her at www.sgbigham.com.

Susi Bocks has self-published two books, *Feeling Human* and *Every Day I Pause*. Currently, she is an Associate Editor at the Fictional Cafe - a virtual coffee shop. You can find her work at IWriteHer.com, where she invites you to read her thoughts and get to know her. Bocks had some of her work previously published at *VitaBrevis*, *Spillwords*, *Literary Yard*, as well as other literary magazines.

Eimear Catherine Bourke is an Irish idealist and perpetual dreamer. Raised in Navan, Co. Meath, she currently lives with her girlfriend in Dublin 6W. Driven by a belief in purpose and fatalism, her poems are shaped by themes such as nature, interpersonal relationships, sexuality and memory.

Dani Bowes is a twenty- two-year-old poet from Baltimore, Maryland. She works as a barista in a small café in her hometown, and prefers tea over coffee. In her free time, she loves watching true crime, listening to Tegan & Sara, and spending time with her sister Megan, and two brothers, Justin and Christian.

Ruth Bowley I do not know how to write a biography. I would not wish to take note of self. Just a simple observer of all things unknown. Of all things worth fighting for. Being a woman, being a survivor, being.

Cassandra Bumford is a 20-year-old from Upstate New York. She currently holds a Bachelors Degree in Psychology, but has plans to pursue a career as a writer. She has one self-published collection, called *To The Left*.

Lynne Burnett lives in the Pacific Northwest. Recent or forthcoming publications include *Arc Poetry*, *Blue Heron Review*, *Calyx*, *Comstock Review*, *Crosswinds*, *Kissing Dynamite*, *IthacaLit*, *Malahat Review*, *Mockingheart Review*, *New Millennium Writings*, *Ristau*, *River Styx*, *Tamsen*, *Taos Journal of Poetry & Art*, *The American Journal of Poetry*, *Underfoot Poetry*, and several anthologies. She is the 2016 winner of the Lauren K. Alleyne Difficult Fruit Poetry Prize, has been nominated for Best of the Net and was shortlisted for Arc's 2018 Poem of the Year. Finishing Line Press published her chapbook, *Irresistible* in March, 2018. https://lynneburnett.ca/

After coming of age in a conservative Christian environment, **Amie Campbell** didn't come fully into herself until she found herself turning thirty, getting divorced, and raising two small children. It was then that she accepted that her love was not limited to one gender and she allowed herself to fall head over heels for a beautiful woman, thinking it would last forever.

Whether it's through tenderness or the passionate or the wistful, **Tara Caribou** adores love. You can find her writing about longing and the heart while outside walking barefoot on an ocean's beach or deep in the cool forests surrounding her home.

Jennifer Carr lives in Santa Fe, New Mexico with her partner and two children. She is an EMT, Firefighter and Poet. When she is not working at the local hospital or firehouse, she spends way too much time reading and writing poetry. Her poetry has been published in print and in on-line publications. Jennifer loves flying by her own wings and looks for any opportunity to soar to new heights.

Laura Elizabeth Casey has been writing poetry off and on for over 3 decades. Her poetry has recently appeared in the San Diego Poetry Annual. She is a graduate of San Francisco State University's undergraduate creative writing program and currently lives in southern California with her wife, dog, and two cats.

Olivia Chachinsky is a first-year college student from Evansville, Indiana, majoring in both English literature and creative writing. She is heavily inspired by the works of modern surrealist and free verse poets such as Lucie Brock-Broido. This is her first published work.

Teresa T. Chappell is a bisexual poet passionate about tethering the unseen onto the material. She is a Princeton in Asia Teaching Fellow and a graduate of Franklin and Marshall College. She graduated with a B.A. in Creative Writing and French Language and Literature, as well as with a minor in Chinese Language. Apart from writing, her favorite hobby is eating (though she was once told that eating is not a hobby).

Clementine is a 10th-grader from Fairfield, Connecticut. She enjoys rainy days, sleeping, music, reading in the horror and apocalyptic genre, and writing!

Kai Coggin is a poet, author, and teaching artist living in the valley of a small mountain in Hot Springs National Park, AR. She holds a B.A. in English, Poetry, and Creative Writing from Texas A&M University. Her work has been published or is forthcoming in *Entropy, Sinister Wisdom, Assaracus, Calamus Journal, Lavender Review, The Rise Up Review, Anti-Heroin Chic, Luna Luna, Blue Heron Review, Hoctok, Yes, Poetry* and elsewhere. Coggin is the author of three full-length collections, *PERISCOPE HEART* (Swimming with Elephants 2014), *WINGSPAN* (Golden Dragonfly Press 2016), and *INCANDESCENT* (Sibling Rivalry Press 2019), as well as a spoken word album called *SILHOUETTE* (2017). Her poetry has been nominated three times for The Pushcart Prize as well as Bettering American Poetry 2015, and Best of the Net.

Carrie Lee Connel lives in London, Ontario, Canada. She has an MLIS from Western University. Her poems have been published in *Synaeresis, The Toronto Quarterly*, and *Phati'tude Literary Magazine*, and two poetry chapbooks: *Persona Grata* (2016) and *A Day in Pieces* (2013), both from Harmonia Press.

Susan M. Conway is an acclaimed fiction novelist, blogger, and mother of two. She resides in Northeast Georgia, where she lives a quiet life. In her spare time, she enjoys gardening and cooking for her family. Susan is a passionate and fiery social justice warrior, mental health advocate, and mentor in the BDSM, Kink, and Fetish lifestyles, striving to empower, embolden, and open healthy dialogues about a variety of social issues.

Selene Crosier lives in lesbian-friendly Austin, Texas. Originally from Saint-Rémy-de-Provence. Her day job involves lots of furry animals. Selene's heart belongs to the countryside, fresh air, kind people and ensuring equality of women. Selene's work is published in many online poetry sites.

Candice Louisa Daquin had the honor to co-edit the hugely successful collection of survivor voices: *We Will Not Be Silenced* (WWNBS) with her Indie Blu(e) sisters, and to a great extent the powerful voices of WWNBS inspired this anthology. Daquin writes for the collectives Whisper & the Roar, Hijacked Amygdala, Free Verse Revolution and Heretics & Madmen. Daquin is the author of five collections of poetry. www.thefeatheredsleep.com

Poet and analytics manager, **Emily Alice DeCicco** was raised in Long Island, NY. She earned her BA from CCNY and her MFA at the Craig Newmark Graduate School of Journalism at CUNY. She resides in the suburbs of NJ with her wife and dog. In her work, Emily explores sensuality, desire, longing and a darker side of oneself. She shares her writing through Instagram (@emilyalicepoetry) and occasionally reads her work at local spoken word events.

Katherine DeGilio is a part-time writer and full-time bisexual from Virginia. You can find some of her previous works in *Soliloquies Anthology*, *Litro Literary Magazine*, *Psych2Go Magazine*, and *November Falls* by Zimbell House Publishing, as well as on fiftywordstories.com and flashfiction.net. She loves connecting with her readers and encourages them to reach out to her on twitter @katiedegilio

Liz DeGregorio is an editorial director living and working in New York City. Her work has previously appeared in *BUST Magazine*.

Grace Desmarais is a queer illustrator and cartoonist currently living in a cozy corner of Eastern Massachusetts. Grace self-publishes auto-bio comics centered around themes of trauma, dis/ability, chronic illness, and art history. Grace's work has been featured in a variety of anthologies including the *Votes for Women Anthology* (to be published

Fall 2020) and her editorial work has been featured in magazines, including *Bright Lite*.

Cristina DeSouza is a poet/physician living in Phoenix, where she writes and practices medicine. She has had poems published in several journals, including *The RAR*, *Sheila-Na-Gig*, *Passaic/Voluspa*, *San Diego Poetry Annual*, *Synesthesia Literary Journal*, *The Healing Muse*. She has a book of poems being released Fall 2019, titled *The Grammar of Senses*. In 2016 she obtained an MFA in creative writing by Vermont College of Fine Arts (VCFA).

M. Duckett-Ireland is a writer, activist, and teacher currently living in Connecticut with her wife and their daughter.

Hoda Abdulqadir Essa is a New Orleans native with roots hailing from East Africa. Hoda is a maker, writer, lover, shapeshifter and soul traveler, searching for heaven or hoping to construct it with her own bare hands.

Melissa Fadul lives in New York with her wife, dog and two rabbits. She teaches English Literature and Advanced Placement Psychology. She loves animals, poetry, and film and photography and baseball and screenwriting. Melissa is currently writing her second poetry manuscript and a screenplay. Melissa hopes that someday she can work with her favorite actresses: Naomi Watts, Rachel Weisz, Cate Blanchett and Mariska Hargitay.

Kirsten Fedorowicz is a lifelong resident of the Midwest who really, really cares about trees. She has been published in *Bisexual Woman's Quarterly* and is a winner of the Academy of American Poets college prize.

Rachel Finch originally started using poetry as a way to accurately express herself after a number of traumatic experiences in her young life. She is the founder of Bruised But Not Broken which was started with the purpose to raise awareness of abuse and provide a place of comfort and support throughout the healing process. She believes that it was with the support of this community that she was able to recover from sexual abuse.

Susie Fought's words have been published in various small collections including three volumes of *BREW*, available on Lulu Press. Born and raised in the San Francisco Bay Area, she now lives with too many dogs in Berkeley, California. www.susiefought.com

Renee Furlow is a poet and spiritual guide from Texas. She has 2 short ebooks on Amazon with the first in a series of Poetry books due out in 2020. Renee can be found on various social media sites as well as her blog at ReneeFurlow.blogspot.com.

Nadia G. is an artist/musician/poet living in Chicago, originally from western MA. Currently she works as a freelancer doing props for TV and film. She is a founding member of the Chicago based post-punk band Ganser. She uses her writing to help develop lyrics and sort her head out. You can find Ganser's music at www.ganser.bandcamp.com Her work has been published by Whisper and the Roar, Sudden Denouement and collaboratively in the music produced by Ganser.

Wandeka Gayle is a Jamaican writer, visual artist, and soon to be an Assistant Professor of Creative Writing at Spelman College (Fall 2019). She has received writing fellowships from Kimbilio Fiction, Callaloo, and the Martha's Vineyard Institute of Creative Writing. She received her PhD in English/Creative Writing from the University of Louisiana at Lafayette. Her writing has appeared or is forthcoming in *Transition*, *Pleiades*, *Kweli*, *Solstice*, *midnight & indigo*, *Interviewing the Caribbean*, among others.

Originally from Cuba, **Milena M. Gil** now lives in Jacksonville, Florida. She writes based on her experiences as a queer, immigrant woman that came of-age in the States. A graduate from the University of North Florida, she now works at an educational non-profit teaching students in under-resourced schools.

Rebecca Ruth Gould's poems and translations have appeared in *Nimrod*, *Kenyon Review*, *Tin House*, *The Hudson Review*, *Waxwing*, *Wasafiri*, and *Poetry Wales*. She translates from Persian, Russian, and Georgian, and has translated books such as *After Tomorrow the Days Disappear: Ghazals and Other Poems of Hasan Sijzi of Delhi* (Northwestern University Press, 2016) and *The Death of Bagrat Zakharych and other Stories* by Vazha-Pshavela (Paper & Ink, 2019).

Mandy Grathwohl is a co-founder of the alternative art and literature magazine *The Matador Review*, where she also coordinates interviews, social media, and development. She is a graduate of Columbia College Chicago's Fiction Writing program. Long ago, she was published in *The Legendary*.

Maria Gray is a poet and writer from Portland, Oregon, currently based in Lewiston, Maine. Her work can be found in publications from the Oregon Poetry Association, National Federation of State Poetry Societies, and University of Portland. She is an Adroit Journal summer mentorship program mentee and currently pursuing her BA in English with a creative writing concentration at Bates College.

Maranda Greenwood is a Vermont poet, she holds an MFA in Poetry from Arcadia University. Her work can be found in *Sundog Lit*, *Slaughterhouse Magazine*, *White Stag* and other journals. In her free time, she collects Zoltar tickets.

Carrie Groebner studied Modern American Literature at the University of Central Florida. She is a lover of words and a lover of autumn as she is fascinated with the way the leaves remind her to let go in the most glorious way. Currently, she is working on a forthcoming novel that blends Astrology and Mysticism with the complexity of love between two deeply artistic women.

V. Hamilton lives in Sacramento, California. She enjoys a career which allows her to travel through California and Nevada. As someone who's newly discovered her love of poetry, she also enjoys all outdoor activities and a diverse and wonderful circle of close friends.

Kim Harvey is a San Francisco Bay Area poet and the Associate Editor at Palette Poetry. She is an alumni of the Squaw Valley Community of Writers. Her poems have appeared in *Rattle*, *The Comstock Review*, *3Elements Review*, *Wraparound South, Typishly*, *Poets Reading the News*, and *Barren Magazine*. She was awarded 2nd Prize in the 2017 Muriel Craft Bailey Poetry Contest and 3rd Prize in the 2019 Barren Press Poetry Contest.

Sophia Healy is a novelist, sculptor and papermaker. Her novels and poems have been published internationally. She taught drawing and papermaking at Bennington College from 1968-1982. Her books *Gobli, Herr Esel & Friends* (Amphibie, 2012) and *Lone Stars* (Atlantic Monthly Press, 1994) are available on Amazon.

Hokis channels zir mistrust in humanity and love for puzzles into unfolding poems. Ze is Senior Editor of "Headline Poetry" @Line Rider Press, and previously served as teacher, community organizer, and body-centered mindfulness coach. Recent works are found in *Truly U*, Paragon Press' *Snollygoster: A Conversation About Politics*, and *For Women Who Roar*. {Hokis; n. /hō/kēs/ The Armenian word for "my soul" or "my beloved."}

Kelsey Hontz is a bisexual Arizonan with a passion for karaoke, the circus arts, and the theater. Her (also very gay) flash fiction has appeared in the zine *It's a Bookmans Thing* and her short story about the time she was hired to portray a domestic violence victim will grace the next edition of *Harpur Palate*.

P. M. Houghton-Harjo is a Mvskoke and Seminole poet and lesbian who resides in New York City and is attending Pratt Institute. She calls Tulsa, Oklahoma her home and has grown to love very red dirt.

Tia M. Hudson lives in Bremerton, Washington, where she teaches English at the local community college. In March of 2019, she was appointed Poet Laureate of Bremerton. Her poems have been published in *The Stillwater Review*, *Ars Poetic*, and *Signals*. Tia enjoys walking with her dog Freckles in the local graveyard.

Hallelujah R. Huston is a screenwriter and wordmistress.

Rachael Ikins is a 2016/18 Pushcart, 2013/18 CNY Book Award, 2018 Independent Book Award winner, prize winning author/artist of nine books. Syracuse University grad, member CNY branch NLAPW, and Associate Editor of Clare Songbirds Publishing House, Auburn, NY. Her new memoir *Eating the Sun: a love story narrative punctuated by poetry and garden recipes* available at https://www.claresongbirdspub.com/shop/featured-authors/rachael-ikins/

Sarah Ito I am a published novelist, essayist, poet and actor. I am an Army veteran and actively involved in Human Rights issues worldwide.

Jessica Jacobs is the author of *Take Me with You, Wherever You're Going,* a memoir-in-poems of early marriage, published by Four Way Books in March 2019. Her debut collection, *Pelvis with Distance*, a biography-in-poems of Georgia O'Keeffe, won the New Mexico Book Award in Poetry and was a finalist for the Lambda Literary Award. An avid long-distance runner, Jessica has worked as a rock climbing instructor, bartender, and professor, and now serves as the Associate Editor of *Beloit Poetry Journal.* She lives in Asheville, North Carolina, with her wife, the poet Nickole Brown.

Paula Jellis was born and raised in Flint, Michigan. She attended Davison High School and went on to earn her Bachelor of Arts degree in Theater at Michigan State University. I have been an out, proud Lesbian for 30 years. I'm one of the few women in the Detroit Stagehand's Union and the only Lesbian. I love words and writing. They are magic and medicine. We are the keepers of our stories our truths. Our history, our present and our future is vibrant, current and powerful.

Carol H. Jewell is a musician, teacher, librarian, and poet living in Upstate New York with her wife, Becky, and their seven cats. She reads constantly, being insatiably curious.

Kelly-Girl Johnston is an autistic writer, visual artist, and coder based in The Bronx, NYC. Kelly's work reflects her neurodivergent perception of time, sound, and social interaction. Much of her time is spent meditating, drawing at the Art Students League, workshopping at Poets House and staring into space. Kelly communicates in Arabic, Farsi, Slovak, Spanish, English and some Front End programming languages. Poems forthcoming in *Blue Mountain Review* and *Amethyst Review.*

Emily R. Jones has resided in Tennessee her whole life. Writing has been her means to express, manage, and make beautiful the emotions that roam through her. Taking the imaginings within her and transforming them into a beautiful array of words is her favorite thing in the world. Writing is both a necessity and a desire to her.

Sarah Kacala I am a survivor of rape and sexual assault, and I am a writer. I have a blog on Facebook to inspire and empower survivors to find their voice again and begin to heal. During my own healing process, I came face to face with the truth about my sexuality and finally found the strength to overcome the religious environment I had been raised in and I came out as gay. I have now met the love of my life and she and I plan on marrying. Finding my soulmate has been the biggest blessing in my life. The most important thing you can do in life is to be yourself; your true and authentic self. It will be the greatest gift you could ever give, not only to yourself, but to the world.

Sarah Karowski is a 26-year-old writer and poet. She has a bachelor's degree in Creative Writing from the University of North Texas in Denton, Texas, and she currently resides with her fiancé and dogs in Tallahassee, Florida. Her work has been featured on *Mad Swirl*, *the Same*, *Sheepshead Review*, *Thimble Literary Magazine*, and she was a runner-up in The Blue Nib chapbook contest. You can find her on most social media as @ladysarahwrites

Nick Kay is a queer Dutch writer, who likes napping, small potted plants, and not sitting normally.

Destiny Killian is a junior English and Liberal Arts double major with a double minor in Psychology and French. After graduation, she has plans to go into the field of editing and publishing. In her spare time, she enjoys writing poetry and learning to play guitar. She loves the little things in life best, including reading, practicing her photography, and having tea with her friends.

Erin King lives in southeastern Pennsylvania. Interests include creating fiber art, jewelry making, and the outdoors. She lives with her partner of eight years.

Crystal Kinistino is a poet and lover of the written word. She has been previously published in *Decanto Poetry Magazine* and Indie Blue's *We Will Not Be Silenced* Anthology. She maintains a feminist blog @ https://medium.com/the-velvet-fist. She is inspired by the works of Virginia Woolf, Sylvia Plath, and Anne Sexton. She is a proud lesbian, radical feminist and half-blood Cree woman residing in the treaty #1 territory of Canada.

Originally from Texas, however, now living in New Mexico, **A. Lawler** enjoys tarot cards, axe-throwing, and writing poetry about failed almost-romances.

Jill Lee. I am a Cincinnati area poet. I currently live with my girlfriend and a cat named Berlioz. I love beautiful things and try to translate them into words.

Aviva Lilith is a queer poet who, like a flower, enjoys the sway of fate. She's been writing since elementary school, working towards earning a BFA in creative writing and photography at the New Hampshire Institute of Art. Along with poetry and flowers, she enjoys knitting, cloud gazing, and dumpster diving for new collage materials.

Tre L. Loadholt is a Writer/Editor located in Southeast US. She has been published in several literary journals, anthologies, and print magazines. She has also published three poetry books; *Pinwheels and Hula Hoops, Dusting for Fingerprints*, and *A New Kind of Down*. Her work can be found at https://acorneredgurl.com and https://medium.com/a-cornered-gurl.

Katharine Love is a psychotherapist and poet. Katharine has just finished her first book, a memoir called The *Lesbian Chronicles*. Katharine currently resides in the resort town of Collingwood, Ontario with her circus puppy Lucille Pearl.

From associate professor of English to management trainer to retiree, **Carolyn Martin** is a lover of gardening and snorkeling, feral cats and backyard birds, writing and photography. Her fourth poetry collection, *A Penchant for Masquerades*, was released by Unsolicited Press in 2019. Find out more about Carolyn at www.carolynmartinpoet.com.

Jennifer Mathews is a self-proclaimed spiritual cheerleader who lives in Mount Shasta, California (or wherever her camper van takes her). Her lifework has included economic justice, laughter yoga, and facilitating conversations on living and dying. In her 2019 TEDx Talk, "Death is Inevitable – Grief is Not," Jen shares how she responded to the death of her life-partner Kate with connection, gratitude, and joy rather than heartache. For more of Jen's writing, go to JenniferMathews.com.

Rachel M. McGayhey (@raymcgayhey) is bisexual, trilingual, and a long-time resident of Tokyo, where she works as a translator. She loves noodles, horror, absurd humor, her native New England, and her supportive husband, family, and friends.

Sean Heather K. McGraw is a historian and adjunct lecturer and received a doctorate in European History from the University at Albany. She has worked as a public librarian and as an NPS Tour Guide. She has published a middle-school textbook, *How the Irish Saved America*, the forthcoming *After Stonewall* and a children's book, *Fiona and the Dragon*. In her spare time, she plays her harp, rescues animals and serves as a member of the Coast Guard Auxiliary.

Lindz McLeod has published poetry with *Wingless Dreamer*, *Passaic/Völuspá*, *Prometheus Dreaming*, *Meat For Tea: the Valley Review*, and *For Women Who Roar*; she was shortlisted for the Fish Publishing Poetry Prize in 2019. Her prose won the Cazart Short Story prize in 2012 and has been longlisted for the Fish Publishing Flash Fiction prize; her short stories have been published by the Scottish Book Trust, *365 Tomorrows*, Dreamscape Press, and more.

Piper Michelle I live in the Willamette Valley in Oregon and much of my work is infused with the nature that surrounds me. I emphasize metaphors in my writing and work to make the mundane surreal by tapping into the fantastical aspects of the natural world. I am passionate about social justice and animal welfare as well as environmental conscientiousness. I aspire to be a therapist and to continue writing and being an advocate

Alexandria Moore is a student at Washington University in St. Louis pursuing degrees in International Affairs, Chinese, and Writing. Alexandria was born in Dallas, Texas and has lived in St. Louis, Shanghai, Amsterdam, and New York. Her work has previously been published in *Armour*, *XMag*, the *Washington University Political Review*, *Sample*, and *Montage*. In addition to writing poetry, she has an affinity for music, greenery, dance, and beekeeping.

Charity M. Muse writes about love between women, social justice, and LGBTQ+ spirituality. In addition to being a writer, she is a speaker, therapist, and empowerment coach, is married to an amazing woman, and is "Momma C" to two wonderful kids. She is currently working on her first novel, tentatively titled *By Heart*. Charity's writing and work as a singer/songwriter can be found at charitymmuse.com.

Skye Myers is a writer and photographer based in Alberta, Canada. She is a Hallowe'en lover, a horror movie enthusiast, and a tattoo addict. She lives in the woods with her darling and their fur babies. Visit her on Instagram @inky.moth or Facebook at Skye Myers Ink-Stained Moth Wings.

Nayana Nair I am an engineer and a technical writer who moonlights as an amateur poet on my blog (itrainsinmyheart.wordpress.com). Writing for me is a process of self-realization and an effort to understand what is ever elusive.

Jack Neece is a passionate woman often consumed by the fire within. She writes to put out the flames. A single mother of four she finds her way through the world with a fly by the seat of your pants mentality and a desire to always say yes to a new situation. Jack lives in small town Ohio with her three sons. A huge culture shock from the fast paced life in Vegas she is used to, but here she is.

Jesica Nodarse is a Cuban-born immigrant living in Florida, with her husband and children. A powerful writer and poet, an intense and driven woman, Jesica offers her unique perspective in today's world and empowers her friends and colleagues with passion and grace. Jesica can be found on Facebook at facebook.com/heathenwordsmith and on Instagram at https://www.instagram.com/j.nodarse/

Michelle Paige is a writer/poet/dyke who lives in Portland, Maine with her girlfriend and two cats. She grew up and went to school in Boston, where she learned to drive aggressively and overcome trauma. She graduated from Suffolk University in 2012 with a degree in English.

Alison Palmer is the author of the poetry chapbook, *The Need for Hiding* (Dancing Girl Press, 2018). To read an in-depth interview by *The Poet's Billow* about the collection visit www.thepoetsbillow.org. Alison's work appears in *FIELD*, *Bear Review*, *River Styx*, *Glass*, *Cream City Review*, *Salt Hill*, *Los Angeles Review* and elsewhere. Nominated for a Pushcart Prize, Best New Poets 2017, and a finalist for Eyewear Publishing's Sexton Prize, Alison lives and writes outside Washington, D.C.

Georgia Park is a contributing editor of Sudden Denouement, founder of Whisper and the Roar, and author of *Quit Your Job and Become a Poet (Out of Spite)*. She has been published in several literary magazines, most recently, *The Offbeat*. She does funny, playful, dark, morbid, Trump related and non-Trump related poems, with or without an emphasis on travel. Read more of her work at PrivateBadThoughts.com

Marie Prichard is a longtime writer and educator. She lives on an island in the Pacific Northwest with her wife, their two wiener dogs, and a Munchkin cat. She loves reading, writing, walking the beach, and filling her wife's pockets with heart rocks.

S. A. Quinox is a young Belgian poetess that loves to display a melancholic and powerful touch in every piece she writes. S. A. Quinox is someone who loves the soul, no matter the gender of the body. She doesn't judge its size, gender, race, etc... And thus she writes for those who struggle to be open in this. You can find S. A. Quinox on Facebook and Instagram for more of her work!

Christine E. Ray lives outside of Philadelphia, Pennsylvania. A former Managing Editor of Sudden Denouement Publications, she founded Indie Blu(e) Publishing with Kindra M. Austin in September 2018. Ray is author of *Composition of a Woman* and *The Myths of Girlhood*. Her writing is also featured in *We Will Not Be Silenced*, *Anthology Volume I: Writings from the Sudden Denouement Literary Collective*, *Swear to Me*, and *All the Lonely People*. Read more of her work at https://braveandrecklessblog.com/.

Talia Rizzo is a lesbian poet studying creative writing at the University of Denver. Her work focuses on her experiences as a queer woman, the complexities of family separation, and the power of images. Talia's work can also be found in *Levee Magazine*, *Foothills*, and *Prometheus Dreaming*. When she's not writing, Talia can be spotted among the Colorado mountains, taking in the sun with the wildflowers or skiing until her legs are sore.

Samantha Renee hails from rural Southeast Missouri and currently resides in Columbia Missouri with her cat Fatimus Solo, who is the true ruler of the home. She enjoys running, and competing in ultra-endurance triathlons and road races. In her free time she enjoys walking Solo on a leash, traveling, reading, and enjoying the process of understanding purpose in the simple moments of life.

Dr. Sneha Rooh is a palliative physician and founder of Orikalankini an organisation that is changing narratives around Menstruation and sexuality in India through art theatre and dialogue. She loves to travel and write.

Rachel Winter Roth graduated from the University of South Florida in St. Petersburg with a Bachelor's degree in English Writing Studies and a Certificate in Creative Writing. She writes for a lifestyle magazine in Cape Coral, Florida *CapeStyle Magazine*, as well as for the entertainment website "Fansided Hidden Remote". Loves horror and wishes to spend eternity writing horror novels.

Maranda Russell is an award-winning artist, author, and blogger who also happens to have Asperger's Syndrome. Her blog (marandarussell.com) focuses on her struggles with mental illness and chronic pain/illness, using her art and writing as a therapeutic way to help heal body, mind, and soul.

Millie Saint-James is a queer writer based in Czechia, though they have lived all over the world, from the velds of Namibia to the metropolis of Osaka. They currently live with their fur son in a one room apartment, performing magic, and writing about queer futures.

Rebecca Sanchez is an undergraduate at the University of Minnesota Twin Cities who is passionate about early childhood education, poetry, and riding motorcycles. In her free time, she enjoys rollerblading and watching Steven Universe. Her work has previously been published in *The Tower*.

SATU is a non-binary interdisciplinary artist based in London, UK. They have recently graduated from a Fine Art degree at Chelsea College of Arts with First Class Honours. As an illustrator, SATU works predominantly with comics and watercolour. They also compose, produce, and perform electronic pop music. The name 'SATU' is Finnish for 'fairytale'. Their latest project, a comic and accompanying EP titled *AN ARCHANGEL*, can be found at https://satu1997.bandcamp.com/album/an-archangel

T. M. Servin, a Colorado native, Tarot reader and energy healer, has always had a passion for writing poetry in particular, and earned a Poet Laureate “many moons ago". She is currently working on publishing her first book; she does not focus on any one subject but instead "writes what I know". Her poetry is energy and nature based, and includes themes of love, self-growth and soul healing. She has two wonderful adult children and a "huge tabby lion" of a cat named Arya. You can find her work on Instagram at @Magicmysticmuse

Kay Shamblin is a lesbian poet, student, and avid D&D player based in Louisville, Kentucky. Her poetry has been published in the *White Squirrel* and *OROBORO*, and her most recent work is centered around body horror, eroticism and intimacy.

Tan Shivers is from Charleston, SC. She started writing poetry at age seven and has been writing ever since. Tan considers poetry to be one of her favorite therapeutic outlets. She recently published her first collection of poetry, *Dark Days Lit Nights – Distant Memories… Up Close and Personal*. Some of Tan's previous work has also been featured in Transcendent Zero Press' *Harbinger Asylum* and the *Rising Phoenix Review*.

Alexandra Short is an emerging writer from Fredericksburg, Va. She graduated from Eastern Mennonite University where she earned a B.A. degree in Communications. Alexandra has also had her work published in an anthology *Virginia's Best Emerging Poets*.

My name is **Izabell Jöraas Skoogh** and I studied creative writing as an international student-athlete at Saint Leo University in Tampa, FL, for a couple of years. I was encouraged by my English professor to continue writing and was later published in the *Sandhill Review Magazine* in 2017 with ”Under the Surface”.

Jamie L. Smith is an MFA candidate in poetry at Hunter College, where she has been the recipient of the Colie Hoffman Poetry Prize and the

2019 Guggenheimer Award, and was runner up for the Academy of American Poets Prize and the Richter Award. She lives in Yonkers, NY.

Janis Sommers I'm an old, working class, sober Lesbian who came out in a rural mountain community in the mid 70's. Life has been a journey that gets progressively better each day. I'm finally writing about it. The poem I submitted has been approved by the woman I wrote about. Now she's writing about it!!

Megha Sood lives in Jersey City, New Jersey. She is a contributing member at Go Dog Go Cafe, Candles Online, Free Verse Revolution, Whisper and the Roar and contributing poetry editor at *Ariel Chart*. Her 300+ works have been featured in *Adelaide*, *Fourth and Sycamore*, *Foliate Oak*, *KOAN*, *Visitant Lit*, *Quail Bell*, *Dime show review*, *Nightingale and Sparrow*, etc. Works featured/upcoming in 20 other anthologies by US, Australian and Canadian presses. Two-time state-level winner of the NAMI NJ Poetry Contest 2018/2019. National level poetry finalist in Poetry Matters Prize 2019. She blogs at https://meghasworldsite.wordpress.com/

Alicia Sophia is a thirty-something punk rocker from Pittsburgh who chased her dreams to the west coast, where she majored in creative writing. She now lives in rural Pennsylvania where she runs on caffeine, obscene language, and still dresses like she did in high school. Alicia has been writing since she was eight years old and has magically transformed into an author. You can find her debut novel *1,4,3 Love, Loss and other Catastrophes* on Amazon.

A. Staley I am a U.S. Army Combat Veteran, a wife, daughter, sister and friend. I care deeply for those around me and try to live my life with no regrets. I have never thought of myself as a writer, but my wife has shown me there is more to who I am than I give myself credit for; that I am stronger, braver, loving, caring and worthy of a soul burning love.

Wil Staley I am a writer, painter, and more. I received my BA in Psychology, MA in Education, and 50 graduate credits in Counseling before coming out; as being queer was grounds for dismissal. I am now seeking my MSW, so I can help those marginalized by society and be a voice for the LGBTQ community. When I met my wife, I knew I had found myself and I'm learning to love the human I have become.

Alison Stone has published six full-length collections, *Caught in the Myth* (NYQ Books, 2019), *Dazzle* (Jacar Press, 2017), *Masterplan, collaborative poems with Eric Greinke* (Presa Press, 2018), *Ordinary Magic*, (NYQ Books, 2016), *Dangerous Enough* (Presa Press 2014), and *They Sing at Midnight*, which won the 2003 Many Mountains Moving Poetry Award; as well as three chapbooks. She has been awarded Poetry's Frederick Bock Prize and New York Quarterly's Madeline Sadin Award. www.stonepoetry.org / www.stonetarot.com

Tekla Taylor is a writer and artist based in Washington, DC. Her work explores history, sexuality, and beauty with a glittering feminist bent.

Shraddhanvita Tiwari hails from Pune, India and holds a Master's Degree in English. A lecturer turned travel blogger, Shraddhanvita has been featured in the anthologies like A *Memento of Feminist Minds* and *Theories of Identity* while her Char works have appeared in *Setu* (Pittsburgh, USA), *Plum Tree Tavern* (Oxford, UK), *Madras Courier*, *Indian Periodical Journal* and more.

Born in Los Angeles in 1946, **Carla Toney** holds a B.A. and M.A. in British and American Literature and was runner-up in the London (UK) Writer's Competition, in 1992. Annie Lennox (Eurythmics) has described her work as "…beautiful, mystical and humane." Denise Linn, Native American author and lecturer claimed, "Carla Toney's poetry is sensuous, lyrical and empowering. It calls down thunder from the heavens to feed the soul." Among others, Carla's work has appeared in *Back Rubs* (Serpent's Tail), *Come Together* (Gay Men's Press), *WiPlash* (Women in Publishing), *Dakini, Big Mouth, and The Likes of Us.* Her historical research, *NoMan's Land: "Multitribal Indians" in the United States* will be published in 2020.

My name is **Charlene Trolinder**, but I usually just go by Char. I'm 35 and for as long as I can remember I've always been deeply attracted to women. I am a soul just trying to live my best life, while doing so compassionately. I have two fur babies, Tinkerbell and Peter. They are my peace and comfort. I first started writing as a way to help ease my depression. Now, I do it because it just feels right. I'm a simple person just trying to live a simple life.

Erin Van Vuren is a Southern California native in love with her girlfriend, animals, and writing. She has been writing since the age of 5, and a professional writer since she was 11. Her goal is to touch as many lives as possible through the power of words. She believes wholeheartedly in the power of imagination and kindness. Currently, she and her girlfriend create art together in California, and push for all young women and LGBT youth to chase and capture their dreams, and know that they are never alone.

Sarah Vermillion. I'm a 27-year-old woman living in Las Vegas, Nevada. I have a love for animals and nature, and tend to take in strays. I like flowers and gardening but can't keep plants alive. I draw, paint, and write. I'm clichéd, overly-empathetic, and a hopeless romantic.

Marvlyn Vincent was born and raised in the Caribbean. She migrated to the United States more than a decade ago, not just in search of a better life, but also to literally save her life. As a child Marvlyn started writing poetry as an escape from the horrors of her reality, but also as an outlet for her pain. This was her way of sharing the things that she could not speak about. Today she still writes about her past experiences, however, she's also developed her writing to include the resolution that has gotten her through the hard times.

Isabel J. Wallace is a queer writer and registered nurse working in the wilds of north Florida. The swamp has left her predisposed towards ghost stories and the certainty that there is always something lurking just out of sight. She has been previously published in *Malaise: a Horror Anthology* from Jessamine Press.

Angie Waters I am a writer/artist who uses the alias A. Shea. A survivor of childhood and adult trauma, my work often reflects my own healing process, especially as a woman. I am grateful to connect with other women working to create a world where we are accepted regardless of our choices or experiences. It is with honor I support every woman in this anthology with two art pieces depicting female empowerment.

Milly Webster is a 20-year-old poet currently studying a degree in English and Creative Writing at the University of Lincoln. She is working on a collection of poetry about bisexual experience and bi-erasure for her dissertation. Further work can be found in the literary magazine *Lemoncurd*.

Vanessa Rowan Whitfield is an American author and artist who currently resides in the east of the states. Her award winning writing has been published in multiple literary magazines and collections, heard on international radio and podcasts and shared at open mics cross country. Growing up with a puritanical family that ostracized the writer for her sexuality, the poet gets a tremendous amount of joy from being a part of any project supporting the LGBT+ community.

Karissa R. Whitson is a nineteen-year-old girl with two cats and a truck. She's been writing since she could hold a pencil and usually doesn't speak to many more people than necessary. She's pretty regular, but can be considered quite astounding, depending on who you ask.

C. E. Wing is a Connecticut Yankee living in the Queen City. A writer and poet. She has dreamed of being a writer since she was a little girl. Her dream was pushed aside for a time but through her journey of self-discovery, she rekindled her passion for writing. She is currently writing a novel, a traditional fantasy with an LGBTQ theme.
https://www.facebook.com/cewingspoems/

To read SMITTEN author interviews and listen to the authors reading their work aloud, please visit https://www.facebook.com/SMITTENwomen/

Made in the USA
Middletown, DE
15 November 2019

78843814R00248